VIOLENCE AND ACTIVISM AT THE BORDER

INTER-AMERICA SERIES
Edited by Howard Campbell, Duncan Earle, and John Peterson

In the new "Inter-American" epoch to come, our borderland zones may expand well past the confines of geopolitical lines. Social knowledge of these dynamic interfaces offers rich insights into the pressing and complex issues that affect both the borderlands and beyond. The Inter-America Series comprises a wide interdisciplinary range of cutting-edge books that explicitly or implicitly enlist border issues to discuss larger concepts, perspectives, and theories from the "borderland" vantage and will be appropriate for the classroom, the library, and the wider reading public.

VIOLENCE AND ACTIVISM AT THE BORDER

Gender, Fear, and Everyday Life in Ciudad Juárez

KATHLEEN STAUDT

UNIVERSITY OF TEXAS PRESS
Austin

Requests for permission to reproduce material from this work should
be sent to:
  Permissions
  University of Texas Press
  P.O. Box 7819
  Austin, TX 78713-7819
  www.utexas.edu/utpress/about/bpermission.html

⊗The paper used in this book meets the minimum requirements of
ANSI/NISO Z39.48-1992 (R1997) (Permanence of Paper).

LIBRARY OF CONGRESS CATALOGING-IN-PUBLICATION DATA

Staudt, Kathleen A.
    Violence and activism at the border : gender, fear, and everyday life
in Ciudad Juárez / Kathleen Staudt. — 1st ed.
       p.   cm. — (Inter-America series)
    Includes bibliographical references and index.
    ISBN 978-0-292-71670-4 (cloth : alk. paper)
    ISBN 978-0-292-71824-1 (pbk. : alk. paper)
       1. Homicide—Mexico—Ciudad Juárez.   2. Women—Crimes
against—Mexico—Ciudad Juárez.   3. Sexual abuse victims—
Mexico—Ciudad Juárez.   4. Victims of violent crimes—Mexico—
Ciudad Juárez.   5. Women political activists—Mexican-American
Border Region.   6. Human rights—Mexican-American Border Region.   7. Police misconduct—Mexico—Ciudad Juárez.   8. Migrant
labor—Mexican-American Border Region.   I. Title.
    HV6535.M43C588   2008
    364.152′3097215—dc22

                                                        2007038705

To the loves of my life:
Mosi and Asha,
my children, now grown, both leaders
in their own ways

CONTENTS

PREFACE AND ACKNOWLEDGMENTS: PATHWAYS INTO RESEARCH AND ACTION AT THE BORDER

Throughout thirty years of teaching and research in political science, my life passions have addressed government responsiveness to women and gender inequalities. Searching beyond policy rhetoric, I focus on policy implementation, or the lack thereof, and on change, drawing on evidence-based research and collective action: women's movements, people's organizations, and professionalism among civil servants for enhanced democracy and good governance. A graduate school mentor, the late Murray Edelman, immersed students like me in "politics as symbolic action," the title of one of his books.

After living in Kenya (1974–1975), where I studied agricultural policy implementation, I analyzed international development policy in gendered technical assistance agencies. I finally settled at the U.S.-Mexico border, where the global and local meet in a comparative political region of cultural mirrors yet economic and political institutional differences. From graduate training in African studies, absorbing knowledge from classics like Frantz Fanon on a dying colonialism, I have become enmeshed in interdisciplinary border studies, to which I believe Fanon can speak on technically dead colonialism but lingering neocolonialism and neoliberal globalization. I have longed to draw on Fanon in my writing, which I do in Chapter 2, but also to challenge his theories about violence and his curious silence on women and masculinities.

In the late 1990s, people in the U.S.-Mexico border region began to hear about horrific, gruesome murders of young women in Ciudad Juárez. Their raped and mutilated bodies were left in the desert. Patterns emerged: victims were young, on average ages eleven to twenty-one; some had breasts cut off and others, carvings on their backs; some were burned, evidently while still alive. Border residents worried about a serial killer or perhaps copycat serial killers. Government officials' public comments soft-pedaled the murders and/or blamed the women for the way they dressed or for being out at night. Victims' mothers, distraught and in mourning, sought justice for their daughters. Instead, the police and investigative agencies treated them rudely, even threatening some of them, rarely pursuing investigations. Locally, the problem was named "femicide" and the murder victims *las muertas*, the dead women, the assassinated.

Increasingly, mothers organized themselves and aligned with coalitions within and across the border, human rights and women's activists among them, to raise awareness, to get justice, and to stop the killings. Activists in other parts of Mexico and the United States networked around the murders, not only human rights groups, but university students and faculty and especially people in performance: theater, music, art, video, and film. Eve Ensler, who wrote and performed *The Vagina Monologues* and authorized its performance worldwide, added a monologue on the Juárez murders and visited the border several times. Eventually politicians and business owners, concerned about cleansing the image of the city, also took steps, all too many of them simply cosmetic. In Mexico, Juárez became a symbol of what people struggle to change: violence, limited democracy, police impunity.

By 2006, many people—especially anti-violence and human rights activists—had become aware of the special stain on the international map symbolized by Ciudad Juárez, Chihuahua, Mexico: the location where more than 370 girls and women were murdered from 1993 to 2003 and approximately 30 more annually thereafter. Immediately contiguous El Paso, Texas, shares the stain, yet it is consistently ranked as the second- to third-safest big city in the United States. Juárez is a complex big metropolitan area with many faces. It is home to several universities; its industrial sector flourishes; its residents compose a broad mosaic of people. Some residents behave with a graciousness long lost in most U.S. cities. Mexico City residents sometimes think that *norteños* (northern residents) have lost their cultural soul, with regional peculiarities more similar to the United States; and Juárez itself has long been understood as a "city of vice," discussed in later chapters. The city is home to one of the world's largest drug cartels; the El Paso–Juárez region is a primary gateway for drugs into the United States, with its huge demand for illegal drugs.

The border has been demonized in the world's eyes, but this is not the complete picture of the border in which I have lived and worked for more than a quarter century. Juárez and El Paso are not as simple as the snapshot that journalists or academic tourists sometimes present. It is my intention in this book to dig more deeply and comprehensively into the big picture, the roots and the commonality of violence against women along with what *fronterizos y fronterizas* (borderlanders) do or do not do about this pervasive violence. I know that men are also victimized by violence—in Juárez hundreds of men are murdered annually compared to the average of thirty women. Unlike victims of femicide, men's bodies are rarely mutilated or raped. The murders of men in Juárez have rightly or wrongly been dismissed as drug-violence killing. While their deaths are also tragic, this book focuses on women victims and survivors; femicide at the border has galvanized the view of Juárez and Mexico throughout the world as a symbolic place of women-killing.

While my lived experience of teaching at the U.S.-Mexico border spans a quarter-century, I have researched the border for fifteen years: informal economies, women in elections, public schools, and cross-border organizing. My journeys have crossed and connected with those of many others, to whom I owe debts of the mind, heart, and soul.

I thank colleagues and friends with whom I've co-authored former work on women and borders: Irasema Coronado, Jane Jaquette, Susan Rippberger, and David Spener as colleagues and friends. Irasema especially shares the commitment to research and action on violence; we have published together extensively. In 2001, when murderers brazenly dumped the bodies of eight women in a field in the heart of Juárez, many of us became active in our transnational, cross-border community. Those eight women suffered the same horrific fate as hundreds of others since 1993. Academics often read and write in their offices, pondering the world or manipulating statistics without connecting their commitments or their work to activists and decision makers. At the border, activism was an imperative. I could only wonder: How could people avoid activism about the deaths? Diana Washington Valdez, a courageous border journalist, had been covering the homicides at some threat to her safety for years, and she published her book, *Cosecha de Mujeres* (Harvest of Women), in 2005 in Spanish and 2006 in English.

I participated actively in the binational Coalition Against Violence Toward Women and Families at the U.S.-Mexico Border, initially co-chaired by Clemencia Prieto, then director of El Paso's Center Against Family Violence, and Emma Pérez, a history/Chicana studies professor, writer, and activist. Inspiring longtime leaders like Esther Chávez Cano of the Casa Amiga women's counseling center in Juárez consistently participated in the coalition, along with members of other nongovernmental organizations (NGOs), activists, and professionals including documentary filmmaker Patricia Ravelo Blanco on more sporadic bases.

Soon, however, it became clear to me that femicide reflected the larger problem of violence against women, not simply by serial killers but also interpersonal violence and domestic violence (I use the two latter terms interchangeably in this study). In 2002, El Consorcio Transfronterizo/The Transborder Consortium for Research and Action on Gender and Reproductive Health at the Mexico-U.S. Border, under the able leadership of Catalina Denman of COLSON (El Colegio de Sonora) and Jan Monk of the Southwest Institute for Research on Women (SIROW) at the University of Arizona, asked me to become part of the network addressing women's broad health and safety issues. I thank them and the consortium, especially Pat Manning, for friendship and colleagueship.

It also became clear to me and others that more research, policy change, and activism agendas would be necessary. I am thankful that my home institution, the University of Texas at El Paso (UTEP), supports partnership with community organizations on both sides of the U.S.-Mexico border. UTEP's Center for Civic Engagement sponsored a workshop for health, nursing, and women's studies faculty from the Universidad Autónoma de Juárez and UTEP, with curricular materials and community partnership opportunities in university classes. And with a large, decades-old NGO in Juárez and its cross-border counterpart, FEMAP (Federación Mexicana de Asociaciones Privadas) and FEMAP Foundation in El Paso, I proposed complex research on domestic violence in Juárez, where no systematic studies had been done (unlike in the United States, with its near-obsessive data-gathering and counting practices). The first proposal to the Center for Border Health Research (CBHR), in 2002, did not score enough points to award funding, as several reviewers sought a more "scientific" quantitative approach.

Armed with reviews, scientific sampling formulas, and other improvements, we proposed research again to the CBHR in 2003. This time we succeeded, and the resources flowed mainly to FEMAP to help make the complex sampling, surveying, and workshops possible. We collaborated over the 2004–2005 funding period to document the incidence of violence and women's strategies to address violence, wondering whether workshops would make a difference in women's perceptions and information about violence (as described in Chapter 3).

How does one come to "know" truths and realities? This is the perennial question of epistemology. My activities went back and forth, from participant observation and activism to scientific research, with insights from each approach tested, developed, and advanced from the other.

Augmenting that, my teaching continued, along with independent study courses with students, some of whom came from the state of Chihuahua. In particular, I appreciated the talents and contributions of Alejandra Martínez, Gabriela Montoya, and Lorena Jiménez. Also outstanding, honors students Mónica Ortiz and Julia Kokina organized a weeklong V-Day conference at UTEP in 2004 that drew thousands of community members into awareness about violence against women. A top-ten senior, Ortiz graduated with university awards for her leadership.

My activism with the Coalition Against Violence continued around many cross-border solidarity events to press for systemic changes in institutions, policies, and social attitudes. With new co-chairs Irasema Coronado, a political science professor and activist, and Victor Muñoz, a retired labor union organizer, and others, we all networked locally on both sides of the border, regionally in both countries, and internationally around various activities (some of which are analyzed in Chapter 4), with parallel networks such as the predecessor Las Cruces, New Mexico–based nonprofit organization Amigos de las Mujeres de Ciudad Juárez. Amigos acts under conditions of courage and risk; I value colleagues Cynthia Bejarano, Gregory Bloom, and Sally Meisenheimer, among others.

On the northern side of the border, those of us who are U.S. citizens carefully avoided any violation of Article 33 of the Mexican Constitution, which prohibits foreign involvement in politics. But we in the coalition have worked with numerous counterpart activists in Juárez and elsewhere to address violence issues on the U.S. side of the border as well. We met with countless journalists and filmmakers from around the world all seeking stories, insights, and contacts; they shared their ideas, insights, and sources with us, and we shared ours with them. As a coalition participant, I also shared perspectives and experiences at universities, professional gatherings, and political venues: the University of California at San Diego, University of California at Los Angeles, Texas House and Senate border committee hearings, Arizona State University West, International Studies and Latin American Studies Associations, and our own El Paso City Council and County Commissioners Court.

I have many more people to thank for their assistance, collaboration, and support on this multidimensional project involving not only complex binational research and workshops but also community action and partnership and the external reviewers. Let me begin with the research project.

Thanks to CBHR, for it supplied two years of research support for a controversial and complex design: six hours of *capacitación* (training) workshops and surveys complete with pre- and post-tests for a total of 615 women ages fifteen to thirty-nine in Juárez. The research partnership involved FEMAP and its research arm, Salud y Desarrollo Comunitario de Ciudad Juárez (SADEC) and the El Paso–based FEMAP Foundation. FEMAP, one of the oldest NGOs in Juárez, enjoys respect from and visibility among residents all over the metropolitan region. Its health clinics, hospitals, nurse training programs, and more than a thousand *promotoras* (outreach workers) have served Juarenses (residents of Juárez) for decades.

·Since the early 1990s, I had worked with FEMAP, especially on its efforts to cross borders, south to north, with its innovative Grameen Bank–like *bancos comunitarios* that provided loans and technical assistance for women micro-entrepreneurs on both sides of the border. In this collaboration, I specifically would like to thank Dr. Enrique Suárez Toriello of SADEC and FEMAP and Vanessa Johnson, formerly of the FEMAP Foundation. Also a valiant journalist, Vanessa Johnson once published the fine weekly electronic *Newspaper Tree*, with its courageous coverage of issues that some print media only take on after *Newspaper Tree* makes the first step.

SADEC professionals Adriana Peña and Graciela de la Rosa facilitated the recruitment of women and the *capacitación* workshops, maximizing participation and voice. The remarkable set of three two-hour workshops, their design, and their execution fell to the able hands of Graciela de la Rosa, a veteran workshop presenter and community organizer. The CBHR also supported half-time UTEP research assistants from Juárez, first Laura Andujo and then Gabriela Montoya.

UTEP's Center for Civic Engagement, under the capable management of Azuri Ruiz, supported student assistance for data entry and analysis from graduate students Amanda Vásquez and Elsa Ontiveros, with much-appreciated guidance from Charles Boehmer for statistical assistance. Technical expert Gabriel Escandón prepared graphics. Before the research began, Guillermo Martínez provided expertise on methodology and Carla Cardoza on design content.

The more deeply involved I got in the research, the more I recognized my need to understand institutional response from the "inside" out. There, the opportunity was in El Paso, where after several decades the police, county, and district attorney's offices developed coordinated responses with nonprofit organizations around support for victims and survivors of domestic violence. In early 2004, I applied to participate in the Victims' Services Response Team (VSRT) of the El Paso Police

Department (EPPD). After passing background and reference checks, I was accepted into the eighty-hour training program, complete with emergency-dispatch lessons and a ten-hour drive-along with a police officer on Mothers Day, one of the most dangerous days of the year for "58s" (the code for domestic violence in emergency dispatch numeric language). As a victims' volunteer, I work with a variety of El Paso women and men, and I thank committed EPPD professionals Gloria Graell and Letty Trejo of VSRT for their inspiring management.

Many others have contributed in countless ways to the insights of this study. Sylvia Rede, a teacher at Bowie High School in El Paso, asked me to collaborate in the school district's ongoing anti-violence training for teens, male as well as female, now ongoing for four years. Leonel Monroy Jr., an excellent professional photographer who covers many community events, donated pictures for this book, as did Aleks Garibay. Photographer Laura Trejo helped with high-resolution scanning and formatting. Susan Hatch is an effective victims' assistance professional connected with the Texas attorney general's office and was my teacher in the VSRT training. Other academics who share my passion for deep knowledge of the Americas or of domestic violence have given me feedback and insights: Howard Campbell, Sandra Deutsch, Núria Homedes, Martha Smithey, and Beatriz Vera. Public officials and their staff members have also put themselves out on limbs on the issue: Guillermo Valenzuela from Congressman Silvestre Reyes' office, Texas state Senator Eliot Shapleigh, and Texas state Representative Norma Chávez.

As I analyzed the data, continuing to move back and forth from research to participation, I made local presentations to health and social science faculty, to domestic violence service providers and officials at their annual conferences, and to the National Latino Alliance to Eradicate Domestic Violence, the Alianza Latina Nacional para Eradicar la Violencia Doméstica. At one poster presentation conference for the border health community, I stood next to my posterboard filled with charts and graphs about the research, ready to answer questions and critiques. What did I remember most about that day? People came to me and whispered questions: Who can be contacted for a loved one in a violent relationship? Luckily, El Paso is home to excellent emergency response services, a coordinated social network, and a twenty-four-hour hotline number at the El Paso Center Against Family Violence (CAFV), which provides counseling and shelter support. I remembered the center's number for those queries whispered in my ear. The royalties from this book will go to the CAFV.

Two CAFV staff members—Cynthia Morales and Aaron Hernández— have been especially good colleagues, for their skill and advocacy and for their assistance in the Center for Civic Engagement's Ni Una Más! (Not one more!) service-learning court observation and high school presentation program. The centers organized fine, condensed, and complex training for university students (and myself) on the cycle of violence, with specialists from the county and district attorney offices. CAFV also allowed me to observe at Battering Intervention and Prevention Program (BIPP) workshops, where abusers talked about confronting "male privilege." I will never forget the adventures Cynthia and I had tracking down details on the benignly named "multiple-use facility" in the state land in El Paso County where sex offenders are imported from outside the region to this for-profit corrections facility.

One month in fall 2005, with all the presentations, piles of documents, materials, clippings, and drafts of these chapters—saturated in details of border violence—I recalled a section in one of my favorite novels, *The Golden Notebook* (1962) by Doris Lessing. Her near-autobiographical character, Anna, surrounds herself with clippings and wonders if she is going mad, organizing the materials and pinning them to the walls to make patterned sense of global conflicts. But, Lessing reflects, "it did not seem to her that she was even slightly mad; but rather that people who were not as obsessed as she was with the inchoate world mirrored in the newspapers were all out of touch with an awful necessity" (651).

Many people at the border and in the heartlands are in touch; they are concerned, committed, and, yes, even obsessed with the scourge of violence against women. I hope this book will deepen insights, commitments, and strategies for knowledge and action here at the border, in the United States and Mexico, and around the world.

For a world without violence!

VIOLENCE AND ACTIVISM AT THE BORDER

Chapter 1

VIOLENCE AT THE
U.S.-MEXICO BORDER:
FRAMING PERSPECTIVES

[O]ther cultures' women-hating practices can obscure the women-hating practices woven into our own cultures.

UMA NARAYAN, IN ORR (2002, 50)

Muerte, el Sabor del Norte *[Death, the flavor of the North]*

FLYER

The world's attention has focused on Ciudad Juárez, Chihuahua, at the northern border of Mexico, as the ghastly, premier center of female homicides in the twenty-first century. For more than a decade, grisly reports and documentaries have emerged about the murders of young women, raped and mutilated before death. Theories abound over who is doing the killings. Some attribute the murders to psychopathic serial killers and gangs. Others decry organ harvesting (the 2003 pretext for the Mexican federal government to intervene). Still others claim that drug traffickers enjoy gang sport after profitable sales. The "sons of the rich," also known as "*los* juniors," have been implicated. And activists persistently raise questions on binational dimensions of the crimes: snuff filmmakers selling to wealthy men in the United States; a handful of victims from the United States; killer-thugs who use border crossing as a way to escape one "justice" system to another; and/or sex trafficking, forced sex work across national borders. Once a feminist issue, sex trafficking is now embedded into nonfeminist post-2000 U.S. foreign policy that categorizes all countries in terms of vague and broad "human trafficking" regulations.[1]

During the past decade in Juárez, the mothers of murdered girls and women have searched for justice with little response from a criminal justice system that is seriously flawed. Activists have joined the search for justice, creating awareness, raising funds, and pressuring governments to respond to violence against women. The result is a broader-based anti-violence movement in North America, where the toleration of violence against women, with a long history, has begun to change.

In a 2003 monograph on female homicide (femicide) in Juárez, Amnesty International counted 370 female murders from 1993 to 2003. Yet Mexican government officials seemed to spend more time quibbling over the precise body counts than investigating, charging, and convicting the killers. Many others have analyzed what has become commonly known as "femicide," from scholars (Monárrez Fragoso 2002; Monárrez Fragoso and Fuentes 2004) to journalists (Benítez et al. 1999; Washington Valdez 2002, 2005a, 2006) and documentary filmmakers (Portillo 2001; Ravelo Blancas 2004a), to name only a few. Although female death totals are constantly contested (over the type of death or probable killers), approximately one-third of the murders involve the rape and mutilation of victims, who are disproportionately poor and young.

What about the border context propels this grisly terror and torture? On Mexico's northern border, Juárez is a huge metropolitan area—Mexico's fifth-largest city—of booming industrial plants, multiple universities, shantytowns at the periphery, obscene income gaps between rich and poor (not to mention between El Paso and Juárez), and home to the Cartel de Juárez, one of the world's largest drug cartels (Campbell 2005; USDOJ 2004). The city has become internationally infamous as the city of femicide, corruption, and police impunity. It is a symbol of Mexico's ongoing struggle for democracy and the rule of law. Consider one of this chapter's epigraphs—a flyer title "Death, the flavor of the North." Distant journalists visit the city to cover only femicide and drugs. A city where 1.5 million people live and work has been demonized, although generalizations about the city and its inhabitants are hazardous. Many in the United States are all too ready to believe the worst about Mexico. Murder and drugs feed stereotypes of the "other" in this post–9/11 world of continuous U.S. rhetoric about security, defense, and terrorism.

With the world's eyes on Juárez, the ordinariness of women-killing in many countries is obfuscated. And with all the focus on the rape and mutilation murder victims, a third of the total presumably murdered at the hands of strangers, people miss the other two-thirds, the girls and women for whom death came at the hands of husbands, boyfriends, partners, or perhaps opportunistic friends or neighbors who transformed interpersonal violence into murders. Domestic violence has become normalized and routine, although it leads to and accounts for some of the women-killing in Juárez, the United States, and other parts of the world. One cannot help but wonder if the public responds only to shock and horror that is dramatized in activism around femicide. All homicides,

Cross symbolizing femicide near a park on Sixteenth of September Avenue, a major Juárez thoroughfare. (Kathleen Staudt)

even less visible but equally horrible "routine" domestic murder and violence against women, should be eliminated. Public safety is enhanced through early public intervention, but over the long term, prevention is necessary to move from the casual toleration of violence against women toward nonviolent cultures.

Several questions prompted me to write this book after many years of research and activism at the border. First, what is the incidence of violence against women (domestic, sexual, and murder) in Juárez, and how can it be explained? Second, how did anti-violence activists frame, prioritize, network, and diffuse their work from Juárez to the border generally and to the national mainstreams? Sociologists who research movement "framing" define it as "interpretive schemata that simplifies and condenses 'a world out there' by selectively punctuating and encoding objects, situations, events, experiences, and sequences of actions within one's present or past environment" (Benford 1997, 415). Third, how do law enforcement institutions respond to violence against women, and fourth, can people learn and apply preventive and protective strategies from one another on both sides of the border?

I argue that violence against women is the overarching problem at the border, and under that umbrella, female homicide. I analyze several explanatory frameworks with a feminist lens, including (1) the global, neoliberal economy and its local manifestations at the border; (2) comparative institutions; and (3) cultures into which feminist and gender power and performance theories are threaded. As I argue in the book, extensive violence against women is attributable to changing gender power relations, especially backlash in the border economic context. But I also attribute high female murder rates to institutional flaws in political and criminal justice institutions, especially in Juárez, Chihuahua. An equally important part of the book involves the analysis of social movement frames, strategies, "frame disputes"—as Benford calls them (1997, 417)—and movement networking and evolution over time. As I describe in the book, social movement activists networked from the border to the world, peaking in 2003 but declining in visibility after V-Day 2004. Yet activists' networking resulted in a broader-based movement that addresses violence against women, albeit with selective, minimal responsiveness from Mexican institutions and still no institutionalized binational approach that addresses the problems at the border.

Here I introduce feminist analyses of global, cultural, and institutional explanatory perspectives and the complex contextual richness of the U.S.-Mexico border, specifically Juárez–El Paso. The border, normally considered the periphery, is at the center in this book, symbolizing struggles elsewhere: about democracy, violence, and impunity. I use "gender performance" as an organizing concept in the book, given its focus on political drama, symbolic politics, and the social construction of gender. I offer a framework for readers that maps social movement connections with the state and government for public policy change toward the rule of law and the eradication of violence against women in binational settings. This framework embraces not only abstract variables from cross-national comparative research but also couples them with in-depth understanding through grounded research methodologies.

Before proceeding, it is important to note that violence against women is extensive in the United States as well as in Mexico. To cross borders with research and action, one must be sensitive to context, carefully grounded interpretation, and the avoidance of making the "other" exotic, as Uma Narayan warns. One must acknowledge not only the difference of institutions in sovereign countries but also the potential similarity of social values and power relations in everyday life. Ultimately, femicide, as Federal Deputy Marcela Lagarde declares (in Morfín 2004, 12), is "a crime of the state," which tolerates the murders of women and neither vigorously investigates the crimes nor holds the killers accountable.

INSTITUTIONS AND CULTURES AT THE GLOBAL BORDER

The border is home to people of Mexican heritage on the whole: most Juarenses and eight of ten El Pasoans, according to the U.S. Census (2000). Seven of ten El Pasoans speak Spanish, and many are bilingual, code-switch back and forth from English to Spanish, or speak a mixed Spanglish. One in four women with partners reports physical violence in the United States and Mexico, but despite these similarities, an average of six times more women and girls are murdered on one side of the border than the other, a number greater than the combined populations of El Paso and Juárez might warrant.[2] Paradoxically, two cities sit side by side, one among the safest and one among the most dangerous in their respective countries.

In this book I utilize several frameworks to understand and explain border violence against women. In political science, the comparative politics field calls attention to governance, political and bureaucratic institutions (March and Olsen 1989; Peters 1999). Political and law enforcement institutions bear on the incidence of crime. Institutions are gendered, absorbing social characteristics of men and women from organizational birth to their current modes of operation (Lovenduski 1998). Quasi-militarized organizations, law enforcement agencies are more male-dominated than most government institutions.

A comparative institutional approach calls attention to rules and routines that shape behavior in the state and its agencies and in organizations and social movements in civil society (Staudt 1997). An institutional lens on violence against women would focus on criminal law, law enforcement, police training and behavior, political commitment for enforcement, and civil society organizations that interact with or avoid the state. Mexico and the United States operate under different governance institutions, legal systems, and rules of law, even though both label themselves federal systems. Laws and law enforcement practices vary enormously. Both countries are sovereign, with governmental authority to make decisions about the people and territory they encompass. People may or may not trust in and use those institutions. Such trust is, in part, a product of democratic processes and professionalism in governance (or their absence). Political institutions influence the national/federal, state/regional, and local/municipal levels in the Mexican and U.S. federal systems of government.

El Paso downtown plaza rally before cross-border march. (Kathleen Staudt)

Institutions in civil society, including social movements and NGOs, amass the potential of "people power" to transform individual or personal problems into public or political issues. Leaders and activists frame issues in new ways, mobilize change, and engage people with governments and other organizations at opportune times (Johnston and Noakes 2005; McAdam, McCarthy, and Zald 1996; Tarrow 1998). In Juárez, the initial core of social movement activism began with mothers of the murder victims and human rights and feminist organizations. Loosely networked alliances grew within and across the border and spread widely and quickly. Global feminist and women's networks shared an uneasy and tentative consensus about the scourge of and priority to eliminate violence against women, but the core frame involved activism against femicide, a shockingly feminized term.

Yet another lens from comparative politics is culture, or the patterns and meanings in people's everyday practices. Culture matters, embracing potentially enormous yet diverse behaviors, attitudes, and historical legacies across generations (Chabal and Daloz 2006). Everyday practices exhibit a range of power and resistance behaviors (Scott 1990). In analyzing Mexico, it is all too easy to demonize men with *machismo*, a bundle of seemingly hypermasculine stereotypes, and thus blame "culture."

Many variations in feminist theory remind one that patriarchy and gender power struggles, whether at the personal level or institutional level, are not peculiar to one culture or to Mexico. Still, it is worth examining gender power and control in Mexico's myths of origin and in global economic contexts (and I do so in Chapter 2).

International approaches begin with the global neoliberal (i.e., market and minimalist state) economic context, the way it shapes local economies, and its generation of inequalities. "Global" also encompasses transnational movements and NGOs that comprise a broader civil society (Ferree and Mueller 2005; Keck and Sikkink 1998; Moghadam 2005; J. Smith 2005). Transnational analysis rarely occurs at borders, with some exceptions (Staudt and Coronado 2002). Tarrow (2005, 11) acknowledges that transnational movement analysis has heretofore given minimal attention to local contexts, a drawback of using solely global approaches. In this book I affirm the global while contextualizing the local.

Mexico and the United States are embedded in the global economy, for better or worse, in interdependent but asymmetrical ways (O. Martínez 1996). Since the Mexican government's Programa Industrial Fronterizo, or Border Industrialization Program (BIP), began in the 1960s to facilitate foreign investment and expanded with foreign export-processing factories (*maquiladoras*) and global free-trade regimes, the border generally and Juárez particularly have become a visible frontline site of the global economy. The city is Mexico's *maquila* capital, home in 2004 to three hundred factories and more than 200,000 workers, over half of them women. For nearly a half-century, the city's history involved a growing, industrializing city of legal freer trade across borders. Border trade also involves illegal drug trafficking and otherwise booming organized crime from the early 1990s onward that is only minimally controlled despite massive increases in both governments' resources.

While the focal period of this study is from the mid-1990s onward, it reaches back to the border of the 1960s, with profound changes in the economy, politics, and power relations: how women and men work and how they organize their public voices. Violence against women entered the public agenda in different ways and eras, with organizing around jobs and wages preceding anti-violence organizing in Juárez. In this book I develop the linkages between economics and violence.

In the Juárez–El Paso borderlands, more than a million girls and women live, but not all of them are well. Some live, even thrive, with security in their homes and communities, with adequate food, shelter, and earnings. Some live in homes free of violence but work in the structural violence of a global economy that has shrunk the real value of earnings in the export-processing economic development model that dominates in Juárez. Still others live in fear and terror: the terror of interpersonal violence, the fear associated with living in a city lacking adequate public security, and fear stemming from the impoverishment of minimum wages that amount to US$4–5 per day, inadequate for safe and healthy lives. Yet others feel freer in a large urban region with wider job options than in small towns, villages, and the countryside: rural domestic violence rates are higher than urban rates, according to national studies in Mexico (INMUJERES/INEGI/UNIFEM 2004). The Juárez border region is special—not rural, definitely urban, and a strange magnet for positives and negatives, opportunity and violence.

Border Theories and Spaces

This study is grounded in the two-thousand-mile-long U.S.-Mexico borderlands, a place where the one-hundred-kilometer radius north and south of the borderline is considered a hybrid region of mixed characteristics and identities. Borders are "in between" places, as theorists, poets, and social scientists have so compellingly proclaimed (Anzaldúa 1987; Bhabha 1994; Staudt and Spener 1998). The border population is large, with many "crossers," exhibiting global economic models and trade including illicit drug trafficking.

The ten border states—four in the southwestern United States, six in northern Mexico—encompass a population of more than 80 million people, but the border region envelops 14 million, according to the 2000 censuses (Staudt and Coronado 2002, 11). My specific focus is on the largest metropolitan region, with more than two million people, to span an international borderline in the world: El Paso, Texas, a city and county of 700,000 residents, and the municipality of Juárez, Chihuahua, with 1.5 million residents. The cities sit together, hugging one another in more ways than their interdependent geography implies.

At the U.S.-Mexico border, analysts and activists deal with the peculiar politics of two cities in two sovereign countries, where people share much in common but live in different economies governed by different institutions. The forces of economic supply and demand, of production and consumption, and of kinship and friendship lock people together in cooperative, complicit relationships. Likewise, Mexico and the United States are close neighbors and trading partners that have enjoyed usually friendly relationships over at least a century.

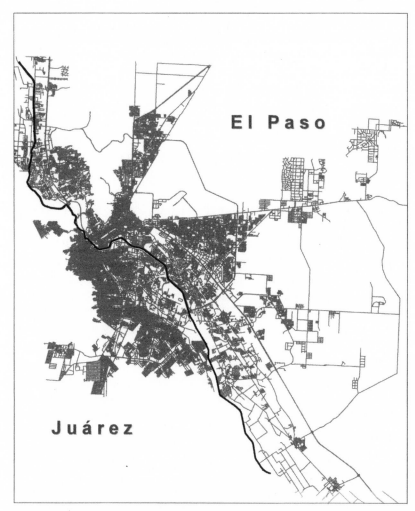

FIGURE 1.1.   *Map of the El Paso–Ciudad Juárez area. Source: City of El Paso Planning Research and Development*

   Prior to the end of the U.S.-Mexican War in 1848, the greater Paso del Norte region was part of northern Mexico. Since then, the area has developed as two border cities growing side by side from a total of 26,000 in 1900 to 253,000 in 1950 to nearly 2 million in 2000 (Staudt 1998, 34). Together, El Paso and Juárez offer a striking example of the difference a nation can make in terms in incomes and minimum wages. U.S. official minimum wages are ten times the minimum wages of Juárez.

Interdependence manifests itself with daily crossings, south to north and north to south, most of them legal. Northbound international bridge traffic into El Paso for 2005 totaled 8,453,000 pedestrians and 16,189,000 cars, many of them carrying more than one person (Fullerton and Tinajero 2005, 14). People cross the border to shop and to visit family and friends. More than 10 percent of the students at the University of Texas at El Paso (UTEP) commute across the border from Mexico daily at Texas in-state tuition rates. At the 2005 Ni Una Más (Not One More) anti-violence conference for 450 El Paso high school students that I moderate annually, approximately 40 percent raised hands indicating that they have relatives in Mexico.

At the frontlines for global economic change, the U.S.-Mexico border became a pioneering test for a neoliberal free-trade regime. The borderline restricts the movement of people and workers separated into labor enclaves of enormous pay differentials, while commerce and goods cross more freely than people. Tariffs that once bound trade were discounted with BIP, based on the value added by export processing. And since Mexico entered the General Agreement on Tariffs and Trade (GATT) in 1986 and the North American Free Trade Agreement (NAFTA) in 1994, free-trade policies have increasingly governed industry and commerce along the border. Free trade has not eliminated U.S. Customs regulations and payments but has added nuances and schedules best understood with counsel from accountants and lawyers (Staudt 1998, Chapter 8).

Global economic forces have altered the contexts within which working people live and earn money. Juárez is a magnet for migrants from towns and states to its south. A once-dominant male workforce gave way to a growing percentage of women workers. Among women, 35 to 40 percent work in the formal labor force; others generate income outside the regulated economy. At the inception of the industrialization program in the mid-1960s, however, maquiladoras recruited far more women (*operadoras*) for their assembly-line operations. In the first phase of maquiladorization, women made up 80 percent of the industrial workforce (Fernández-Kelly 1983). Through the second and third phases as factories diversified (Kopinak 2004), a far larger, more gender-balanced workforce peaked at 250,000 workers, spawning new, imaginative social constructions of gender within diverse factory settings (for example, see Salzinger 2003). Even though massive changes occurred in the workplace, gender ideologies have not caught up with the different economic base (Staudt 1986), giving rise to the male backlash that I analyze in Chapter 2.

Violence at the Border

The frontier location stimulates crossing for what is quaintly called "vice," whether it is illegal on one side and not the other or enforced more effectively on one side than the other. RAND researchers Peter Reuter and David Ronfeldt note that "Mexicans have always been available to supply whatever Americans want but cannot obtain legally in their own country—just as Americans have always been ready to provide whatever Mexicans want and cannot acquire readily in Mexico" (in Andreas 2002, 196). Current demands at the border involve drugs (for the United States) and guns (for Mexico).

Juárez was the city to which people crossed southward for alcohol (during U.S. prohibition), prostitution (as sex work is regulated, not outlawed), and divorce (prior to the passage of U.S. no-fault divorce laws; O. Martínez 1978). In contemporary times, Juárez is widely perceived as a "city of vice": Pablo Vila's narratives (2005) portray the city as highly sexualized, dirty, violent, decadent, and corrupt.

The border is a key drug trafficking gateway, and Juárez has undergone a seeping "cartelization." Like Tijuana, it is home to drug-transit operations that grew once the U.S. war on drugs shifted the Colombia connection from Miami to the long U.S.-Mexico border. The enormous amounts of drug-money profits, skyrocketing since the early 1990s, generate corruption and collusion with officials (Andreas 2000). José García notes that "at one point 90 percent of the police officers, prosecutors, and judges in Tijuana and the state of Baja California were on the Arellano Félix payroll . . . [and] the cartel pays up to US$1 million a week in bribes to law enforcement officials" (2002, 322).

While media attention often focuses on drug "lords," it is important to understand the broad networks of mid- and low-level players in drug marketing and distribution, especially in areas with high unemployment and poverty rates. El Paso is one of the five poorest big cities and one of the three poorest counties in the United States. Howard Campbell's research shows the ubiquity of drug trafficking as a normal, everyday part of life in the border region. In El Paso, he says, "trafficking is a practical, quick way poor people can increase their incomes" (2005, 327).

Drug consumption is higher in the United States than in Mexico (J. García 2002, 304), and the prospect for legalization (and greater control) is dim. When the U.S. war on drugs is effective (the exception rather than the rule), drugs are stuck in Mexico, likely dumped at lower prices and thereby spreading drug use in Juárez.

Tattered poster depicting a young girl crying reads: "In a present [time] of horror, your silence and fear consent to a future of impunity." (Kathleen Staudt)

In paradoxical contemporary times, the border-as-drug-corridor has been coupled with a dense network of national agencies that police the movement of people and goods, whether legal or illegal and documented or undocumented. The border has been "militarized" (Dunn 1996) yet with a drama and spectacle of "border games" (Andreas 2000) and irregularities among police agents on both sides of the international line (Bowden 2002).

With the mix of "bordering and debordering" (Spener and Staudt 1998), along with new laws and policies that since 1994 have facilitated more trade in legal commerce, freer trade in illegal commerce is omnipresent. Former U.S. Drug Enforcement Agency (DEA) employee Phil Jordan called NAFTA a "deal made in narco-heaven" (in Andreas 2002, 203; also see Payan 2006a,b). Investigative journalists have identified the hunting of young women for rape and disposal as a form of drug-cartel "sport" after big sales (Corchado and Sandoval 2004a).

Violence against women is a global problem, and the scale and scope of global legal and illegal trade and production contribute to the scourge, as do urban size and growth, migration, inequalities, and anonymity in big-city life. As a high-growth industrial region, northern Mexico be-

Flyer in a window on busy Juárez Avenue, with the familiar Se busca *("Looking for"), conveys her family's anguished search for a missing twenty-two-year-old schoolteacher. (Kathleen Staudt)*

came a magnet for people seeking a more prosperous life in a place of glaring contrasts between rich and poor in Juárez and El Paso. Paradoxically, Juárez and the state of Chihuahua have a higher per capita income than most states in Mexico, while El Paso's per capita income is only 60 percent of U.S. per capita income (Staudt and Coronado 2002).

Historically the border is a legendary and lawless periphery that outlaws cross for safe haven. Criminals still cross in the twenty-first century, including men who hide after being charged with domestic violence and murder. Occasional consumers cross with wads of cash but no visible means of support, paying for cars or houses without paper trails. The border is not only a place of transnational activism but also an escape valve.

Criminals' escape across the border makes tracking them and investigating their crimes difficult. After all, Mexico and the United States, two sovereign countries, are at work, each with its own set of criminal justice institutions. Even victims cross the border seeking higher justice standards. The vignettes that follow came from extensive news clippings (with surnames omitted) and from participant observation.

- In 2005, Maria Luisa was found beaten, strangled, and stuffed in the closet of a home, but her alleged killer, ex-boyfriend Richard, fled to Mexico.
- A U.S. Marine recruiter was shot in Juárez. The high-tech surveillance camera installed by the new state Preventive Police was turned upward, rendering it useless in identifying the perpetrator on the video.
- David, who reported his cousin's killing in Chihuahua City, was in southern Mexico when she died, but after police torture in prison, he confessed and was convicted of her murder. Women in Black, an international NGO, mobilized appeals for justice, and border activists pleaded for justice on appeal with the Mexican Consulate in El Paso. David was assigned a fifty-year sentence but released in 2006.
- On the sidewalk in front of Casa Amiga, a nonprofit organization that counsels battered women, a woman was murdered by her ex-husband in 2002. He was tried, convicted, and served time in prison but allegedly used political clout to seek early release. With a letter-writing and email campaign, activists on both sides of the border convinced the state of Chihuahua to deny early release.
- Battered women cross into El Paso seeking safety at one of thirty-one homeless shelters. They report husbands threatening to kill them and leave them in the desert without fear of investigation. El Paso County

Attorney professionals cannot easily serve offenders with notice about protective order hearings—a civil law remedy—once abusers cross.
- El Paso County Sheriff's deputies warned callers at a semi-rural home who phone 911 on multiple "58s" (domestic violence): "If you call again, we'll report you to the Border Patrol." This is not supposed to happen with federal legal protection to undocumented domestic violence victims.

In late 2006, binational and national killings and crossings made headlines. One of the alleged killers of the eight young women brazenly dumped in a cotton field inside Juárez in 2001, galvanizing much activism, was identified in Colorado and transferred to Mexico. An El Pasoan was killed by her live-in boyfriend who crossed the border, hanged himself, and was later identified by Mexican authorities.

Despite seeming lawlessness, an atmosphere of lawfulness and civility also prevails. Binational cooperation and cross-border organizations operate in many areas of commerce, trade, water, and civil society interests (Staudt and Coronado 2002). At the national level, scores of treaties specify details about air traffic control, insect infestation, and drugs. At the local level, police departments have long cooperated over stolen cars. While human rights treaties abound in the Americas and internationally, there is no U.S.-Mexico human rights treaty. Nor had local police cooperated over femicide until 2003, when regional anti-violence activists called for cooperation around female homicide at least on a par with auto-theft cooperation.

After pressure from anti-violence activists, meager cooperation began for such matters as training on evidence preservation at homicide sites and a toll-free tip line in Spanish and English for details about the serial killings. Lately, more official requests for cooperation occur. When in 2005 the authorities located the body of an eight-year-old girl buried in cement after sexual assault, the Chihuahua state attorney general requested U.S. FBI profiling assistance from its Quantico, Virginia, database. A sex offender profile matched, leading to identification. Activists called for a binational Amber Alert–type quick response to binational child kidnapping, but sovereign governments maintain their separate ways on sex offenders, one counting and registering them and the other using the same routines as for other crimes.

Borders are special, hybrid places where binational, cross-border solidarity, government cooperation, and action are necessary to address public problems in a common region. Given the global economic context

Flyer featuring the photo of a murdered girl offers a reward for "information leading to the capture of my murderer(s). I WANT JUSTICE!!"

for extensive legal and illegal trade, cooperation is warranted, even in a U.S. political context that stresses walls, fences, and defense. Violence epidemics may be more common in a metropolis like Juárez, where anonymity and a perception of big-city vice can prevail. The global-local border locale cheapens labor, and people's earning capacity is linked to capacity, self-worth, and the ability to exit dangerous relationships.

In Chapter 2 I will discuss gender as socially constructed performance, and such performance is dazzlingly patriarchal, as demonstrated
in a close reading of Mexican intellectuals like Paz and Bartra. I develop
the argument that the construction of "masculinities" at the border
has not caught up with change among women who resolutely denounce
violence—as I document in Chapter 3—but who cannot easily exit abusive relationships. Some men become violent when threatened with loss
of power and control, meager as control may be in the general economy
and the private household.

GENDER PERFORMANCES

Political drama is a central organizing theme in this text. Governments
and activists produce drama with outcomes both symbolic and real
(Edelman 1964, 1971). Symbolic politics are vivid at the U.S.-Mexico
border. Social movement analyses highlight the importance of frames,
drama, performance, and media spectacles (Benford 1992; McCarthy,
Smith, and Zald 1996) for expanding the base of support.

Popular culture emits mixed messages about violence against women,
whether in newspapers, films, art, music, the Internet, and television or
from social movement frames themselves. Violence against women is a
constant, embedded theme in popular culture. Its portrayal is rarely neu-
tral but rather emerges in one of two orientations: critique or celebration.
The combination of sex and violence titillates some. TV dramas and mov-
ies focus excessively on violence against women, suggesting prevalence
far more common than actual numbers and thereby generating a "politics
of fear" (Glassner 1999). In U.S. crime shows of the past decade, police
perform as dutiful investigators of violent crimes, although Mexican television (transmitted across the border on several channels) offers little by
way of their own police and crime dramas. However, newspapers on both
sides of the border dwell on lurid tales of murder and death. Through the
mid-1990s, reports in Juárez impugned the victims' reputations (Rojas
Blanco 2006), but after that, with social movement activism and its criticism of police impunity, the tide turned in media reports on femicide.

Worldwide, women and feminist activists organize against violence,
one of the few issues about which South-North consensus exists, across
class, nationality, and ethnic lines. United Nations conferences, from
the 1975–1985 International Decade of Women to the 1995 Beijing conference and subsequent gatherings, resolve to eliminate violence against
women. Keck and Sikkink (1998) show the rapid spread of this compel-

ling, priority transnational issue for women. Popular culture and the media spread awareness about violence that titillates and warns, that evokes fear and outrage, that evokes emotion and empathy. Dramatic representations arouse emotions that allow social movement activists to communicate with broader publics (Cadena-Roa 2005; also see Benford 1997; Goodwin, Jasper, and Polletta 2005). Given the commonality of violence, few women's lives are untouched by such knowledge, whether from partners, parents, strangers, or their own personal experiences.

To change policy and society, activists and policy advocates must generate awareness and build support for systemic, concrete changes among constituencies and multiple groups, the broader the better (Stone 1997). Anti-violence activists have used drama, testimonies, films, and plays to frame and extend their messages. Performance is a useful concept around which to analyze anti-violence social movements at the border. In literal and figurative performance, activists have spurred the development of constituencies that press governments for change.

I will begin with performance as literal and concrete. Consider decades of street theater, films, and plays, including *The Vagina Monologues: Until the Violence Stops.* Playwright and activist Eve Ensler began a global campaign to call attention to violence against women, female sexuality, and other long-dormant issues once part of the 1960s–1970s women's movement in Mexico and the United States. V-Day in February, often February 14, evokes several images and symbols: violence, vaginas, and/or Valentine's Day. The celebration of V-Day calls attention to violence on a global scale; in 2004, women performed in 2,300 *Vagina Monologues* worldwide in 1,100 cities (www.vday.org). Baumgardner and Richards, in their book on grassroots feminist activism (2005), note that those plays and accompanying activism "have exposed more people to feminism than any other entity in the last decade" (177).

Performance can also be conceptualized in figurative, less concrete terms. Philosopher Judith Butler analyzes gender as performance, as historically performative (2004, 30); "how one does gender" is also a lens through which one can understand violence in context: at the border. Women and men perform gender in socially constructed ways. Violence is embedded in language and in behavior; it is learned. Moreover, activists and social movements "do gender performance," using drama and performance with symbols, icons, colors, wrenching and emotional testimonies, and stories. Symbols can help build movements and expand constituencies. Interactive performances occurred among NGOs and governments with the use of numbers, maximized and counted over a decade, while the Mexican government responded with minimizing and contesting numeric counts. As Deborah Stone has analyzed so well (1997), "numeric metaphors" are common in symbolic politics.

At the border, anti-femicide activists have communicated, silently and loudly, with the use of symbols and colors: crucifixes, pink and black crosses. They painted names and colors on crosses, dresses, and public signs. Activists mourned silently in public, setting symbolic political stages for anti-violence activities. Victims' mothers and activists repeated stories, showed pictures, and gave personal testimonies at rallies, creating vivid memories with personal names and faces attached to them. At various levels, Mexican government officials disputed the numbers or trivialized the totals as crimes of passion or normal domestic violence.

Of course, violence on the border is not only about symbols. Death and violence are real. Many women and girls have died; many more have been injured and threatened. Fear has been engendered into everyday life.

In analyzing gender as performance, Butler offers seeds of hope with her conception of regulation and reregulation. Butler reminds readers that gender practices are regulated through social norms and that common practices normalize behaviors and interactions (2004). Violence against women is all too "normal" in gender interaction. Anti-violence activists challenge the normalization of violence, reframing it instead as abnormal and no longer (if it ever was) legitimate. Butler's discourse evokes questions about a new form of regulation, one that deregulates gender injustice and uses gender-fair law to reregulate, to shame, and/or to criminalize previously "normalized" interpersonal violence as pathology.

FROM CROSS-NATIONAL TO GROUNDED APPROACHES

At the U.S.-Mexico border, violence against women derives from and symbolizes flawed governance and criminal justice institutions, whether the violence involves more than a decade of femicide and its hundreds of victims or the everyday domestic violence and tens of thousands of survivors. Whether at the border or elsewhere, violence against women is an exposé of the state, masculine privilege embedded therein, and unequal gender power relations in state and society. The exposé is reiterated in the media from local to national and global on daily bases. State unresponsiveness to women is advertised. The exposé has penetrated people's awareness and consciousness to create multiple climates—of fear, of disgust, of anger.

Governments and policies can and do change, sometimes in response to public pressure, problem documentation, and the dysfunctions and costs associated with protecting those who injure, maim, and kill. Cross-national analysis offers a focus on institutions and cultures with testable hypotheses that can be connected to government responsiveness.

Cross-National Analysis: Why Governments Respond

S. Laurel Weldon, in *Protest, Policy, and the Problem of Violence Against Women* (2002, 23), uses a cross-national approach to compare thirty-six countries that according to Freedom House rankings were continuously democratic from 1974 to 1994. The United States is one of those countries. Looking at the protest-to-policy relationship, Weldon methodically analyzes factors that influence governmental responsiveness to the problem of violence against women (13–17); I group the indicators she uses into five categories:

- Legal reform for wife battering and sexual assault
- Crisis centers and shelters for victims of battering and sexual assault, along with government funding for those services
- Training about violence against women for police, judges, and social workers
- Preventive public education
- Central coordination of national policies on violence against women

Weldon explores four possible explanations for the adoption of responsive policies and practices, all of them with numeric or categorical indicators for statistical analysis: culture, ideological orientations that frame policies, and development levels; women's and social movements; women legislators; and governmental institutions such as women's bureaus that the United Nations calls 'women's machinery.'

Contrary to popular notions, Weldon found culture, ideology, and development levels to be poor predictors of government responsiveness to violence against women. It made little difference whether countries were rich or poor, leaned ideologically left or right, or exhibited intensely religious or hypermasculine, hegemonic character. Costa Rica, with a lower per capita income than many other countries in the comparison, was among the most responsive. Nor did high percentages of women in legislatures or the presence of women's machinery in government make a difference for responsiveness to violence against women. Rather, Weldon found that pressure from civil society, especially women's and human rights activists, explained policy adoption far more than other factors.

Deepening Comparative Analyses at Borders

Where might Weldon's analysis leave comparative border analysis? Institutional response to domestic violence is far greater in the United States than in Mexico and in El Paso greater than in Juárez. But analysis must go deeper, from the ground up. A grounded approach confirms some of Weldon's conclusions but also locates further refinements and new variables, especially if binational governance is to be responsive (Figure 1.2).

But first I review Weldon's variables of ideology and development. The U.S. gross domestic product is approximately four times that of Mexico (UNDP 2003). Minimum wages at the border exhibit more glaring inequalities, with a tenfold difference. And as noted earlier, Juárez is considered relatively well-off in the Mexican context, while El Paso's per capita income is just three-fifths of the U.S. average. But again, money alone does not make the difference, as Costa Rica has shown. The United States and Mexico pursue neoliberal, market-driven approaches to trade and economic development, with constitutional prohibitions against collusion between church and state. These variations provide little ability to predict responsiveness here, as Weldon would agree.

Consider also women in politics and women's machinery in government. Women have much better prospects for election into Mexico's national legislative bodies. Mexico exceeds global averages in the proportion of women in national assemblies, while the United States falls below those averages (IPU 2007); however, the reverse is true at state and local levels (Staudt and Vera, 2006). And Mexico has far more women's machinery in government at centralized and state levels than does the United States, with its mid-level Women's Bureau inside the U.S. Department of Labor. In Mexico's response to the United Nations' routine queries about the Implementation of the 1995 Beijing Platform for Action (INMUJERES 2004b), remarkably complex programs are described that would seemingly provide multipronged attention to violence against women, although Juárez has felt few ripple effects. Like Weldon's analysis, these factors do not take one far.

Women's movements are visible along the border and in both countries (Evans 2003; V. Rodríguez 2003). Beginning in 2001, media stories on women in Juárez and El Paso reported through the lens of women's and human rights NGOs. Yet Mexico's institutional response to violence against women is meager and more symbolic than real. Regardless of how women's and human rights organizations flourish in both countries, NGO relationships with the authorities differ. Mexican activists, who tend to be cynical and wary of co-optation (with good reason), interact less with government institutions and mainstream political campaigns. Thus, even with Mexico's outsider NGOs and insider women, the government hardly appears more responsive to violence against women. The qualitative engagement with the state by social movement activists and NGOs warrants analysis.

Other details about both countries are worth noting, including indicators amenable to cross-national analysis. Mexico ratified the 1979 Convention on the Elimination of All Forms of Discrimination Against Women; the United States has not. U.S. women won the right to vote in 1920, more than thirty years before female enfranchisement in Mexico in 1953. Neither the era of the women's vote nor treaty signatures predict differences in government responses to violence against women.

Weldon's framework assumes that the rule of law exists in democracies and that professional standards of accountability prevail in bureaucracies. Most scholars and activists would classify Mexico as democratizing or in transition to democracy. But Mexico does not exhibit the rule of law, and its criminal justice institutions perform poorly (Bailey and Chabat 2002a; Domingo 1999; HRW 1999). Citizens express widespread mistrust of the police. Police officials have low stakes in reducing crime and crime rates, and few bureaucratic incentives exist to investigate crime (Zepeda Lecuona 2002). The United States and Mexico take very different approaches to justice.

With the opportunity to pursue grounded border analysis in this study, I expand Weldon's broad and abstract cross-national analysis for deeper explanations about the response or lack of response to violence against women at the border. I examine the considerable differences between the United States and Mexico, Texas and Chihuahua, El Paso and Juárez, all hosting relevant institutions within federal systems of governance. To explore meanings more deeply, I turn to grounded analysis that draws on multiple methods to learn from the context.

Multiple Sources and Methods: Grounded Analysis

This book builds on cross-national insights to address violence against women at the border through grounded analysis that gains insight from deep knowledge of the border context and its institutions. Grounded analysis is holistic and relational, aiming to learn from context and understanding through field experience. It moves from deductive to inductive understandings, from quantitative to qualitative methods, using a mix of methods and sources. The researcher describes her participation transparently (Naples 1998, 7).

I have drawn on multiple methods—quantitative and qualitative, participant observation, rich secondary sources (published and unpublished), and a large sample of women ages fifteen to thirty-nine in Juárez. The research builds on participant observation and activism based on *compromiso*, that is, commitment to the community. As Irasema Coronado and I more fully outline (2005), researchers' *compromiso* "transcends friendship to ensure that the research in some way benefits or addresses the cause" (145). As Nancy Naples says about ethnographic work (1998, 6), my goal is "to produce a narrative that retained the integrity of the specific events, actors, and context while revealing the broader processes at work."

I have woven together many concepts and perspectives, drawing on decades of research on women and gender, institutions and bureaucracies, and the border. Over the past four years, the research became more specialized and focused on violence against women. The analytic movement back and forth was continuous and constant. To formulate these ideas in a "logical, systematic, and explanatory scheme," I used many angles and perspectives in an interplay of inductive and deductive thinking and of methods that allowed the emergence of explanation during the research process, or what Strauss and Corbin call "grounded theory" (1998).

I have been active in the Coalition Against Violence Toward Women and Families at the U.S.-Mexico Border since its inception in 2001. The coalition illustrates one among many cross-border organizing efforts by people who join forces around common interests that transcend the borderline in this binational metropolitan region (Staudt and Coronado 2002).

Collaboration was built into the research. Edleson and Bible define collaborative research as "investigative partnerships between advocates, practitioners, social scientists, community activists, and women" (2001, 74; also see Bojar and Naples 2002). Partners included the El Paso Center Against Family Violence, public schools, and FEMAP.

In the quantitative research, I collaborated with FEMAP, a large NGO, and its U.S. support organization, the FEMAP Foundation. Women participated in workshops that facilitated active learning, discussion, and small-group projects that produced informative posters, and their voices emerged in an otherwise mechanical, quantitative research project. The content of women's posters revealed their keen awareness of violence, its multiple causes, and the numerous strategies necessary to overcome violence. Women provided answers to many research questions about the incidence of and risks associated with violence. Other qualitative research complemented and deepened more comprehensive understanding of domestic violence.

A Border-Grounded Framework

Drawing on grounded theory, this book offers a framework to examine the connections of social movement and NGO activism and government responsiveness (or lack of it) to violence toward women at the border. The model is not intended to reinvent social movement theories but rather to provide a roadmap for this book and the missing pieces of the puzzle to connect activism with government responsiveness on both sides of the border. The model unpacks some of the interactive relationships deemed necessary to facilitate social movement activism to broad-based NGOs and government, with accountability and oversight relationships from outsiders (civil society) and insiders.

The model in Figure 1.2 posits the interplay of external/outsider and internal/insider activists and strategic players in building and broadening the base of pressure to protect women, to intervene early after conflict, and to prevent violence against women. Broad-based responsiveness emerges from multiple institutions, not merely law enforcement but also nonprofit organizations and civic oversight. The sources of pressure on government are numerous, from outsiders to insiders, from external to internal activists. The external outsiders who bear on public agency responsiveness include feminist and human rights activists and mainstream associations in the business and economic, nonprofit, faith, education, and health sectors. Men also join these efforts. With changing popular culture, dramatic education expands with music, novels, art, and film.

Outsiders interact with insiders, or those in government who also pressure decision makers in the public system with the capacity to budget for and sustain programs that protect women, intervene against perpetrators, and prevent violence: women decision makers who control budget strings in federal governance, women's machinery, and legislative bodies are more likely to take the lead before their male counterparts in pressing for responsiveness, even though men and women share interests

Eliminating Violence Against Women: Border-Grounded Framework

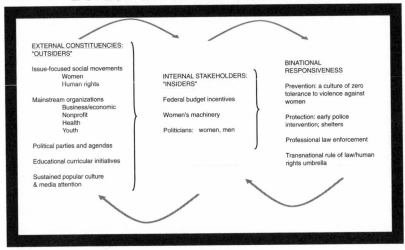

FIGURE I.2. *Binational Border Framework*

in protecting mothers, sisters, wives, and daughters. However, women legislators have never been the majority in the political system of Mexico or the United States.

For governments to respond to violence against women, several conditions are necessary: free press, rule of law, and professional accountability. Border media provide sustained coverage of murder and violence, allowing activists to count the victims and develop an evidence base to promote change. Law enforcement differs across the border, each side with its own flaws, but one side invests little energy into professional investigation. Vividly framed activism displays symbols and dramatic gender performances that make systemic deficiencies memorable. Governments counter with equally symbolic actions, but they are far more powerful and far better funded than the activists. What makes the border context special is the binational scope of the problem, the ease with which criminals cross to elude justice, and the absence of an overarching human rights agreement with concrete, accountable mechanisms that respond to violence against women. Once-local networking that grew enormously over a decade must be sustained in ways that connect to the United States and Mexico and the binational responses necessary to address violence against women.

ROADMAPS IN THIS BOOK: OUTLINE OF CHAPTERS

The book contains conceptual, empirical, and strategic analyses of interest to multiple audiences concerned with violence, borders, activism, and women and gender. Chapter 2 presents a review of existing knowledge on violence against women from global to local perspectives. In it I analyze cultural and global studies that deepen understanding of border economic changes over the past half-century, joining seemingly disparate but coherent connections from Octavio Paz to Frantz Fanon and Hannah Arendt and ultimately to masculinity studies that speak to the border.

Chapter 3 draws on the representative sample of women who participated in workshops and completed surveys in collaboration with FEMAP in 2004–2005. I report on the climate of fear and the reality of violence, on the incidence of physical and sexual assault, and on the risks associated with that violence. Tapping insights in women's posters from workshops and survey responses, I further consider women's own analyses of the violence and the strategies they use in response to it. Data from the survey challenge cultural notions of women in Juárez as submissive to and compliant with violent behavior.

Chapters 4 and 5 of this book focus on comparative institutions in the U.S.-Mexico border region. Chapter 4 spotlights civil society, including a wide range of social movements and NGOs that make violence against women dramatic and visible. A core NGO base in human rights and women's organizations networked with distant and wide networks, peaking in 2003–2004, expanding anti-violence constituencies in civil society thanks to electronic communications, a relatively free press in Mexico and the United States, and the press' perceptions of its readers as having insatiable hunger for murder stories. One part of civil society performs popular culture and performs with drama: music, art, film. Those activists magnified and heightened the dramatic presentation of horror stories with colors, icons, and images. Subsequently, the economic establishment invested sporadic commitments to eradicating violence, with perhaps more attention to the border's image than to substance. Many border people built a wider base to foment cultural and organizational changes to reduce the social toleration of violence against women. Much work still remains to be done.

Chapter 5 looks at government institutions that can and should respond to violence against women. Public institutions are the slowest sector to change in ways that would address the violence epidemic. In the chapter I look specifically at whether protection from violence against women is available, from where, and whether public intervention occurs early enough to forestall the spiraling momentum of often-worsening violence. Once women report violent crimes, a host of public and private responses are possible, not only from the police but also in the nonprofit sector and the courts. The chapter reveals flaws on both sides of the border, with huge challenges that result from bureaucratic tangles.

In the conclusion, Chapter 6, I rethread all these lines of analysis with strategies and possibilities for change. I also warn of the significant obstacles to change, not the least of which involve the economic violence and harsh drug and human trafficking so visible at borderlines yet seeping across other borders into mainstream societies.

Violence produces injuries with multiple consequences, thereby evoking the need for action and policy change. This research is conducted in the spirit of hope and faith in democracy and in reasoned policy analysis. Will authorities use evidence to address public health and safety problems, including violence against women? Historically, class and gendered analyses offer doubt for affirmative answers to these questions. While Mexico and the United States claim the label of democracy, functioning political practices have muted the voices and agendas of many women and of economically marginalized people in general for much of the history of each country.

Amid grim narrative and cynicism about delays and obfuscation, this book coincidentally exhibits the politics of optimism. On one side of the border over a span of thirty years, pressure for responsiveness on violence against women produced changes toward early intervention and prosecutorial action on domestic violence as crime. The other side of the border delays such action with defensive posturing but cannot afford to wait any longer if injury and death to women are to diminish and finally end. Yet even with early public intervention, strategies are hardly in place in either country to change a culture that tolerates violence against women—even death—at exorbitantly high rates.

Fronterizos and *fronterizas* are aware of the daunting challenges associated with change, including the alleged collusion among authorities and segments of the super-rich (including drug cartels). However, people are engaged in struggles for democracy and rule of law that is fair to women and men. Many people invest considerable time, talent, and risk in this movement: human rights activists, professionals in health and public safety organizations, attorneys, and feminist and labor organizations. This is their story.

Chapter 2

CULTURE AND GLOBALIZATION: MALE BACKLASH AT THE BORDER

[E]very decrease in power is an open invitation to violence.

—HANNAH ARENDT (1959, 87)

Violence against women has touched most people in the world, through their own experiences or those of their mothers, daughters, sisters, and/ or friends. Violence against women occurs in many forms, from rape, sexual assault, and battering to psychological and verbal attacks including threats and intimidation.

Sexual and other physical violence is now considered a crime in most civilized countries. In some countries, even verbal and psychological conflicts are legally actionable, but those forms of violence leave less evidence and make prosecution difficult. Conflict is the product of social learning, that is, failures in learning to interact with respect, responsibility, and accountability. Criminal violence is overwhelmingly male-on-female, while verbal conflict is equally shared, at least in the United States (Straus 1990).

Violence against women has been magnified as a border problem due to the widespread international attention to the murders of girls and women in Ciudad Juárez. Consequently, attention to domestic violence and homicides resulting from it has been muted, although this terrifying but "normalized" part of everyday life is found not only in Juárez but around the world. Border social movements have framed and prioritized the hundreds of femicides, coupling numbers with grim and horrifying testimony from victims' mothers about shockingly irresponsible police behavior. In so doing, activists initially missed the opportunity to stress the ordinariness of everyday violence against women and its victims and survivors. While analysts and activists are attentive to "opportunity structure," they must also consider "missed opportunities" (Meyer, Whittier, and Robnett 2002, 17). In this book I do not miss the opportunity to link femicide and domestic violence.

Here I examine violence against women, grounding global and cultural perspectives at the border. In reviewing conceptual, definitional, and methodological issues in relevant studies, I analyze how violence against women has become so common as to call it "normalized" behavior in the Americas. A closer look at cultural studies then allows a better understanding of the contexts and symbols that perpetuate violence at the border. I tread into the cultural territory of gender power relations and the defensive, oppositional backlash generated among a minority of men who "perform" gender apart from legality and women's discourse, neither of which legitimizes nor tolerates violence.

Violence against women is a relic of male dominance, legitimized by government policy or government inaction until the latter part of the twentieth century. Government inaction represented policy, that is, a hands-off policy on violence within households. As Smithey and Straus starkly say (2003, 245), "the marriage license was a kind of implicit hitting license provided there was no serious injury" (also see Robles Ortega 2005). Yet even after domestic violence was criminalized, its practice has persisted on a massive scale.

DEFINING AND MEASURING VIOLENCE AGAINST WOMEN

The World Health Organization (WHO) defines "intimate partner violence" as behavior that causes physical, psychological, or sexual harm to partners in a relationship; these behaviors include:

Acts of physical aggression, such as slapping, hitting, kicking, and beating
Psychological abuse, such as intimidation, constant belittling and humiliation
Forced intercourse and other forms of sexual coercion
Controlling behaviors such as isolating a person from family and friends, monitoring a person's movements, and restricting a person's access to information or assistance (WHO 2002, 89, my emphasis).

Governments typically define physical and sexual violence as illegal, for such violence provides evidence that makes intervention actionable. I define and measure physical violence in this book's analysis, including rape, beating, slapping, and other actions.

Violence has multiple psychological consequences on its individual witnesses and survivors, such as depression, anxiety, fear, and apathy. The 1995 World Mental Health report linked broad societal upheaval and debilitating poverty to increased alcohol and drug abuse, suicide, and violence against men, women, and children. In the context of chaotic modernization, rigorous economic restructuring, and political violence, a vicious circle emerges wherein "violence begets violence" (Cohen, Kleinman, and Desjarlais 1996, 13–15). Although weapons like knives are easily available, the widespread presence of firearms enlarges the threat of harm, especially in the United States, with easy access to guns. The former U.S. Surgeon General considered firearm access a public health problem of the late twentieth century, when more than half of homicides involved firearms (ibid., 14; also see Glassner 1999).

VIOLENCE AGAINST WOMEN: "NORMAL" IN THE AMERICAS?

Research on violence against women, once nearly invisible, is now voluminous. Government statistics and academic research document the extent of violence, but one should exercise caution with regard to how numbers are presented (Ruback and Werner 1995). Moreover, definitions differ, time periods vary, and the use of different survey questions may lead to over- or underestimating actual conditions. Ultimately, most statistics rely on reported rather than actual violence, and underreporting is a chronic problem in government statistics and even in survey self-reports.

Analyzing the Americas (the Western Hemisphere), Mayra Buvinic, Andrew Morrison, and Michael Shifter report (1999, 3) that "30 to 50 percent of adult women with partners are victims of psychological abuse, while 10–35 percent suffer physical violence." WHO (2002) similarly reports on statistics in two large cities in Mexico, Guadalajara and Monterrey. Violence is learned, and studies throughout the Americas "document a strong connection between victimization in childhood and later involvement in some form of interpersonal violence" (Buvinic, Morrison, and Shifter 1999, 10). On income differences, Gonzáles de Olarte and Gavilano Llosa (1999) note that the rich guard their privacy well, but poverty aggravates the "tensions of daily life and increases the likelihood of violent behavior" (34), tripling rates compared to the wealthy (39). Caroline Moser and Cathy McIlwaine argue that "poverty and inequality frequently overlap to generate conditions in which some people resort to crime and violence" (2004, 13).

In the United States, report rates have increased over the past twenty years (Smithey and Straus 2003), but many victims still do not report crimes to the police. Even to researchers, respondents may be reluctant to acknowledge violent experiences, given the shame and pain. Still, one in four women with partners reports domestic violence (USDOJ 2001). The National Violence Against Women Survey in 2000, drawing on samples of 8,000 women and 8,000 men in the United States, found that 25 percent of the women respondents and 7.5 percent of the men had experienced rape and/or other physical assault by a partner, but few of the crimes were reported to police: 20 percent of the rapes and 25 percent of other physical assaults (NIJ/CDC 2000). A three-city study of low-income Hispanics in the United States (Frías and Angel 2005) found more than one in four women reporting abuse and the highest rates among people of Mexican heritage compared to those from Puerto Rico and the Dominican Republic. The researchers found that citizens were more likely to report crimes than immigrants, at least among low-income Hispanics. Undocumented immigrants are vulnerable and less likely to call attention to their households.

In Mexico as well, the incidence of violence ranges from a quarter to a half of women, when defined and measured in broad, inclusive questions that combine psychological and physical violence. A massive Mexican representative study of 57,000 households in eleven states (INMUJERES/INEGI/UNIFEM 2004) found that 47 percent of women experienced a wide range of abuse—physical, sexual, emotional, or economic—within the previous twelve months, whatever the women's educational background. More rural women (12.2 percent) than urban women (7.6 percent) reported physical violence within the previous twelve months.

At a minimum, a quarter of women with partners on both sides of the border have experienced physical violence. However typical these shocking figures, so common that they seem normal, the violence is not only illegal but also results in short- and long-term damage to victims in physical and psychological terms, to their children who observe and sometimes reproduce violence in adulthood, and to lower economic productivity because of lost workdays. Moser and McIlwaine (2004) call violence a "development" issue. A study sponsored by the Inter-American Development Bank documents economic losses plus hospitalization and medical costs in Mexico City (Lozano Ascencio 1999; also see the national study of hospital admissions, INSP 2003). Lozano Ascencio reported that "five of every ten women who sought treatment at the hospital emergency departments surveyed presented injuries stemming from marital disputes" (1999, 88). He categorizes the damage (89):

[The] most frequent physical injuries are contusions, superficial injury, and ecchymosis (bruises) on various parts of the body. The areas of the body most frequently injured are the face (55 percent), upper limbs (43 percent), and lower limbs (37 percent).

Lozano Ascencio found that intrafamilial violence usually produced injuries that were considered slight in legal terms, healing in two weeks or less. While legally slight, however, wounds that last for weeks are significant. Mexican women are at risk for violence during pregnancy (Larraín 1999, 109; Freyermuth Enciso 2004; Valdez Santiago 2004b), findings not unique to Mexico.

Many Mexico-wide studies have limited value for local use and application at the border because they are only disaggregated to the state level. Until this book, Juárez lacked methodical research on domestic violence.

Evidence: Femicide Versus Domestic Violence

Female homicide numbers provide more complete evidence of violence against women, if bodies are located. Activists called attention to many female disappearances, but no certainty exists about death or relocation, whether voluntarily or involuntarily, perhaps as human trafficking. Juárez female homicide numbers hover at thirty annually, while El Paso counts five or less, despite the prevalence of shared Mexican heritage for most people in the border region. The contrast calls into question simplistic notions of *machismo* as a cultural explanation, which I address in greater depth later. But gender power conflicts, often grounded in economic distress, are also cultural unless tempered with public-safety institutional intervention that reduces violence.

In the drama of border anti-violence movements and government reactions, numbers became "metaphors" for critiques and challenges (Stone 1997, Chapter 7).[1] Activists usually cite 1993 as the beginning of femicide (Rojas Blanco 2006), and government statistics show dramatic rises in the rates of male murders per 100,000 population (49 to 100) and female murders (6 to 23) in a one-year period of 1992–1993 (COLEF 2006, 279), a time frame that coincided with the rise of drug trafficking.

NGOs in Juárez view official Mexican government figures with suspicion, and I share that skepticism after tracking femicide over the years. Police lose murder reports, evidence goes missing, cases are mysteriously closed or solved, and the number of mutilation-rape female homicides changes depending on which party controls state government.

Even fine agencies like INEGI depend on homicide reports from the tainted criminal justice system, with its Orwellian qualities. Juárez is a numeric outlier for female homicides, but the effort to analyze precise figures is an exercise in futility. In Juárez, human rights organizations maintain the most methodical list, based on an accumulation of press reports validated by victims' families. Without an increasingly free press, widespread killing would be less visible.

I believe that the murders and everyday violence should be understood as interconnected. Violence against women is the overarching problem, whether by partners or strangers, serial killers or opportunistic predators. A dead woman represents a tragic death, regardless of who committed the murder. Good, professional law enforcement intervenes to protect victims, prevent homicides, and hold perpetrators accountable.

In examining the normalized violence against women in the Americas, it would be prudent for readers to unpack reports with regard to definitions (broad versus narrow), periods covered (ever experienced? experienced in specific periods such as previous weeks, months, or years?), sampling methods, sample population, and geographic locations studied. My domestic violence research based on a sample of women in Ciudad Juárez suggests that 70,000 women have been at risk for physical violence yet live in a city where few trust the police and a minimal number of safe shelters exist.

CULTURAL PERSPECTIVES ON VIOLENCE AGAINST WOMEN

Anthropologists have analyzed interpersonal violence in broad and deep perspectives. Among the broader views, the books of Peggy Sanday (1981) and David Levinson (1989) stand out for their methodical, cross-cultural perspectives. Sanday, examining scores of micro-societies, identified connections between warlike behavior, environmental scarcity, and violence against women. Levinson found "wife beating" to be the most common form of family violence, present in 84 percent of the ninety micro-societies he examined. Yet it was rare or nonexistent in other micro-societies he analyzed that had more economic equality between men and women, equality in monogamous marriage and divorce, and intervention in domestic disputes by people outside the home. From these broadly comparative studies, one can conclude both that violence against women is connected with the larger society and that it is amenable to change, depending on economic contexts and public intervention.

Weldon's (2002) cross-national analysis of thirty-six democracies is also testimony to such change.

However, these broad studies of micro-societies rely on dated ethnographies stored in the Human Relations Area Files (www.yale.edu/hraf), an archive founded in 1949 of all world regions based not on nationality but on subnational peoples living in a world with changing national borders. Those societies analyzed near the U.S.-Mexico border included Mescalero, Tarahumara (actually Rarámuri), and other peoples whom contemporary social scientists might term "indigenous" or Native American. It would be a serious stretch to generalize from these studies to larger-scale mainstream societies. Over the twentieth century, these peoples' incorporation into societies and economies subjected them to national and state laws that influenced indigenous norms. Moreover, people from these areas have migrated to cities and across borders. Historical perspectives reveal extensive movement and change.

Mexican Historical Perspectives

Historically, physical and sexual violence against women has not been criminalized in Mexico, particularly when the perpetrator was an acquaintance or intimate partner, related through family, or resident of the same household. As patriarchy modernized in mid-nineteenth century Mexico, legal intervention was possible if men failed to control excesses, without motivation, against women whose honor and morality were undisputed (Alonso 2002, 128). In Varley's class analysis (2000), Mexico's 1871 criminal code discouraged "crude" male behavior.

Historical anthropological studies provide insight into "culture," or the symbols and webs of meaning that are selectively passed on from generation to generation and that frame everyday behavior (Chabal and Daloz 2006, 23–25). Several philosophers address Mexican myths of origin with a heavy emphasis on gender. I begin with the best-known philosopher to address culture (or "national character"), Octavio Paz, revered by some, critiqued by the empirically minded (Wilkie 1984), and analyzed as a "handful of stereotypes codified by intellectuals" as a "hegemonic political culture" (Bartra 1992, 2). Then I move to the classic analyses of anthropologist Oscar Lewis, who pioneered the use of life stories to understand families in rural and urban Mexico through the mid-twentieth century. To the extent there is intergenerational transfer of abusive behavior (Ferreira-Pinto, Ramos, and Mata 1998; Moser and McIlwaine 2004, 110), his work is relevant.

Mexico's Character: Hegemony?

Whether he perpetuates myths or portrays "national character" with sharp brilliance, Octavio Paz speaks to gender constructions and violence. Drawing on history, conquest, and colonialism, he invests a full chapter in *The Labyrinth of Solitude* (1950, reprint 1981) on "The Sons of Malinche," with Malinche as the alleged *traidora* (traitoress), La Chingada, during the Spanish conquest.

Paz delves into the origin and meanings of *chingada* from the Aztecs, the Spaniards, and Central and South America. In Mexico, he says, the word suggests many meanings, shades, and emotions: aggression, violent wounding, sexual violation without consent. "The *chingón* is the *macho*, the male; he rips open the *chingada*, the female, who is pure passivity, defenseless against the exterior world . . . in a relationship determined by the cynical power of the first and the impotence of the second" (77). Men and/or "the Mexican" are *hijos de la chingada* (in crudest terms, children of the fucked one). Here Paz moves in universalist Freudian directions: "We are alone. Solitude, the source of anxiety, begins on the day we are deprived of maternal protection . . . these feelings are common to all men" (80). His work reads like a historical justification for and anguish about violence against women, against the mother or wife who abandoned and/or betrayed the son or husband.

Another philosopher updates such analysis and frames it as hegemony. Roger Bartra has a whole chapter on gender construction in *The Cage of Melancholy* (1992) that he titles "*A la Chingada.*" To understand Mexican identity, says Bartra, one must understand two seemingly incompatible myths: the virgin mother, the Guadalupana; and the raped fertile mother, La Chingada, Malinche (147). The archetypical Mexican woman embraces the duality of the "Chingadalupe" (160).

The subtitle for Bartra's book is *Identity and Metamorphosis in the Mexican Character*, stressing change but calling into question what is or was real and what morphed and became a cage that trapped identity. Like Paz, Bartra moves in psychoanalytic directions. One section of Bartra's chapter, worth quoting at length, addresses "modern feminine duality"— Guadalupe and Malinche, "two sides of the same coin . . . that the national culture has devised":

> The cult of the Virgin of Guadalupe is seen as a deep expression of man's guilt, whereby he begs forgiveness from the woman he himself has betrayed and abandoned; love for the virgin runs in parallel with worship of the mother, now institutionalized but practiced only

under certain circumstances and on special occasions. But Mexican man knows that woman (his mother, lover, wife) has been raped by the *macho* conquistador, and he suspects that she has enjoyed and even desired the rape. For this reason, he exerts a sort of vengeful domination over his wife and expects total self-sacrifice from her. Thus arises a typical sado-masochist relationship. (158)

Bartra criticizes myth-making as a hegemonic project that intellectual elites foisted upon people, men and women alike, as traits of national character. Myths and symbols may be woven into people's consciousness as explanations for their behaviors. These myths not only portray men as brutes but women as masochists—both clearly over-generalized and at odds at least with the evidence in this study wherein the majority evinces the absence of these behaviors and attitudes.

Other analyses purport psychological insights about interpersonal violence that may be relevant to the cross-generational transfer of abusive behavior. In his now-dated book on men and culture, Samuel Ramos (1962) stresses men's violence as a mask for their inferiority. Another dated psychoanalytic study (Fromm and Maccoby 1970) reports men with narcissistic traits and women with masochistic traits. Both feminist and masculinity studies challenge the Mexico-specific quality of these generalizations, and critics of Freud may dismiss them as well. However, the vividness of Paz and Bartra and the extent to which they weave men, women, and violence into discussions of real or hegemonic character suggest that culture may bear on the gender power relational change that has occurred at the border over the past half-century of multigenerational learning.

Across Generations: Culture in Oscar Lewis

Few anthropologists of Mexico have been popularized as much as Oscar Lewis, perhaps with a hegemonic-like quality, however dated the original field research. Like other fact finders and myth makers and conveyers, his work is relevant, especially for understanding the intergenerational transfer of abusive behavior.

Lewis collected autobiographies in the 1940s and 1950s utilizing tape recorders, a new technology of those times. He focused on extended families and solicited rich, deep, thick description of everyday family life through respondents who narrated lengthy stories that spanned generations in post-revolutionary Mexico. Lewis represented families as "typical," situated in and from Central Mexico rather than the north, such as

the state of Chihuahua or the other five border states. The characteriza-
tion may be relevant, for many Juarenses have migrated from Central
Mexico, and the life stories reflect the consequences of multigenerational
learning in the lives of residents' parents or grandparents. Three of Lewis'
books (1962, 1963, 1964) offer potential insights on domestic violence.

In *The Children of Sánchez* (1963), Jesús Sánchez and his adult children
provide vivid memories of the different stages of their lives to illustrate
everyday urban poverty, while *Pedro Martínez* (1964) and his family's stories represent rural poverty. Both books have what Lewis describes as a
Rashoman-like quality, with family members voicing different memories
of themselves and/or their fathers and mothers. Stories reflect constant
change and flux. For example, while Jesús Sánchez is "domineering and
authoritarian," his children born between 1928 and 1935 are exposed to
"post-Revolutionary values" that emphasize "individualism and social
mobility" (1963, xxiii).

Drawing on memories, family members thickly describe domestic
violence, from husband to wife, parents to children, and siblings to siblings. Violence is so omnipresent as to be normal, yet it is remembered
vividly. However, fathers present themselves as men of authority who
argue, while other family members remember these arguments as fright-
ening violence. The fathers themselves do not evoke violence in their
presentations of self. Mothers are presented as subservient and submissive with husbands but angry about men's infidelity and their violence in
disciplining children.

In *Five Families* (1961), Lewis presents a panorama of what he calls typical families, from the desperately poor Gutiérrez family to the newly rich
Castro family. He weaves life stories into family interaction and memories over a day. Adult women are resourceful with money, occasionally
earning money informally and keenly managing their allowances from
husbands. An exception is Isabel Castro, who totally depends on her rich
but abusive husband. The Gutiérrez family, Lewis says, "comes closer to
an equality of status and power between husband and wife than any of
the other families, and significantly this is the only one in which the wife
is a major economic support of the family" (17–18). Yet in all five families,
husbands beat wives. Even Pedro Martínez, committed to the ideals of
revolutionary social justice and later to intense religiosity after his con-
version, does not apply these beliefs to his relationships with women.

What do Oscar Lewis and these family life stories have to contribute to understanding Ciudad Juárez? Mexican anthropologist Lourdes
Arizpe has said that "Mexicans learn authoritarian patterns within their

families, unquestioningly accepting the authority of their fathers" (in Turner and Elordi 2001, 158). Yet change is constant, and the near-universalism of intrafamilial violence in Lewis' minuscule sample appears to have lessened in the late twentieth century to the extent that survey results reported earlier in this book are valid. Still, Ruth Behar's research (1993) presents the life story of one woman, Esperanza, as threaded with interpersonal violence. But one woman is surely not typical. Moreover, Behar raises doubts about Esperanza's presentation of her history as well as anthropologists' representation of "realities."

Cultural continuities can be analyzed in different institutional contexts in migration studies, two of my prime interests in this book. Few such studies focus on violence, but Jennifer Hirsch's research (1999) is an exception. She analyzes cultural changes across generations and boundaries in her life histories of migrants from semi-rural northwestern Mexico to the urban southeastern United States. In particular, Hirsch compares previous and emergent values in marital relations. Companionate marriage patterns, she says, emerged in Atlanta, and the incidence of domestic violence decreased due to women's access to the police, the vulnerability of abusers' undocumented status, and women's greater ability to support themselves economically should they exit abusive relationships. Thus, one can conclude that cultural values are tempered by situational and institutional contexts. Pablo Vila's narratives from Juárez also add insights about marital power dynamics in U.S. institutional contexts. One of his informants, Robustiano, was "astonished that his acquaintance had to spend six months in jail simply for following the Mexican custom of showing who has power in a marriage . . . : 'Six months in jail just for slapping the girl' " (2005, 139).

Migration studies permit cultural comparisons in different institutional contexts. While domestic violence has not disappeared in the United States by any means and much violence goes unreported, Hirsch and Vila show masculinity culture at odds with leverage that the rule of law and institutional intervention generate for victims of violence. Such findings emphasize the greater importance of institutions for explaining violence against women.

Perspectives from Contemporary Juárez

Thus far, I have considered explanatory perspectives on violence at the border involving cultural, institutional, and global factors. Here I connect the Mexico-wide research reviewed earlier with the specific context of Juárez. At the border, violence is not a universal experience for women, with one of four women reporting physical domestic violence and about one in ten reporting sexual assault. This does not square with the families whom Oscar Lewis taped. Perhaps Lewis did not identify "typical" families, or perhaps his stories are dated, although cross-generational continuities pass on seemingly dated practices. Or maybe power relations within families have changed as women have begun to earn money and acquire respect or generate mutual economic dependency within households. There is considerable research on whether women's independent earnings influence power dynamics in households, with mixed findings. In the research of Benería and Roldán in Mexico City (1986), among women who earned money through home-based work, even meager earnings gave them leverage or allowed them to exit dysfunctional relationships. Still, children learn from parents who settle conflicts between themselves or with their children in sometimes violent ways. Corporal punishment in families is also relevant.

Corporal punishment is common in the United States, as Straus documents extensively (1991); and research in the state of Sonora in northern Mexico documents "harsh parenting" (Frías-Armento and McCloskey 1998). In Juárez, FEMAP/SADEC did a study of economically marginalized *colonias* (neighborhoods) with a sample of 981 youths ages twelve to nineteen. Nearly a quarter of the sample reported physical assaults by parents or another adult in their homes over the previous two years. More male teens (28 percent) than female teens (18 percent) reported victimization. The report summarizes about parental violence that "for each physically abused woman, 1.6 men are beaten" (Suárez Toriello, de la Vega, and Parra 2000, 15). The researchers write that, contrary to their expectations, parental violence increased with the age of children. They explain this by the urgency of physical violence "when parents are faced with the inability to solve or control" their children's behavior and attitudes (16). Besides violence as learned and reproduced behavior, as many studies suggest, perhaps vulnerable boy victims digest a sense of resentment and a will for revenge against women—revenge that emerges in violence against women during adulthood. The confluence of culture and global conditions must also be understood in the border context.

Mexico's northern border is situated at the frontlines of the global neoliberal economy, which generates economic growth and wealth for some but inequalities and impoverishment for many others. Globalization is only one of many drastic economic, political, and demographic changes that have taken place over the past century. As a nation, Mexico moved from an agrarian to an urban industrial economy, from rural to urban population majorities, and from one-party to multiparty democracy (however compromised such democratic models can be for women). Mexico, once colonized, moved to independence and through revolution to a compromised sovereignty under neocolonialism and subsequent globalization.

Part of Mexico's profound change involves the rise of female participation in the labor force, which changes the balance of power within households. In Juárez, women's formal participation in the labor force rose rapidly in the 1960s and 1970s with the Border Industrialization Program and the growth in export-processing factories where women comprise more than half the workforce. Yet the ideology of male family breadwinners prevails despite the reality of impoverished workers, men and women (Staudt 1986). Many men are less able to contribute to household maintenance and perhaps more likely to become abusers. Duvvury (2002) cites "failed masculinity" to explain violence against women.

Because Mexico's complex changes are linked to the global economy, the following analysis in neocolonial contexts offers insights that connect violence against women with male backlash in gender power relations. From many potential authors, I examine two preeminent analysts: Frantz Fanon on violence in neocolonial contexts and Hannah Arendt on violence. While neither has much to say about women, both discuss power at length. I interrogate them with a gender lens and examine masculinity studies in Mexico. The analysis sets the stage for understanding male backlash in gender power relations.

Global Perspectives

In his magnificent and eloquent classic, *Wretched of the Earth* (1963), Frantz Fanon provides a sweeping analysis of the late colonial era in Africa and Asia, an era of structural violence that degraded those whom Fanon called native peoples. The longest of his essays is titled "Concerning Violence." Fanon, from Martinique, crossed oceanic boundaries to North Africa, where he first worked in a hospital with psychiatric patients and later joined the nationalist movement in Algeria's struggle with entrenched French settler colonialism.

Fanon shifts back and forth across the Atlantic, referring to the expanse of the area now called "the South" and its low-income national economies (in contrast to the wealthy "North"). In three essays in *Wretched of the Earth* he discusses the pitfalls of national consciousness,

highlighting the ways in which class and race become embedded in political parties that replicate the power concentration and hierarchy of
former colonial masters. Mexico's post-revolutionary political hegemony, especially seventy-one years of one-party domination, epitomizes
Fanon's analysis of the pitfalls of national consciousness.

In *Wretched of the Earth*, Fanon only addresses gender in off-handed
ways, making reference to the perpetuation of feudal male-female relations in the colonial and post-colonial eras (203). From his analysis of
Latin America, colonized far earlier than Africa or Asia, he provides fore-
boding warnings. Fanon even acknowledges or anticipates the globalized
sexual and trafficking industries; he criticizes the "delicious depravities"
in the exploitation of "little Brazilian and Mexican girls, the half-breed
thirteen-year-olds" (154), using crude language himself. Mostly Fanon
unintentionally offers insights about masculinities.

For Fanon, violence begins with the structure of colonialism. Although he later criticizes feudalism, and specifically the "feudal tradition
which holds sacred the superiority of the masculine element over the
feminine" (203), Fanon does not discuss male-to-female violence. His
silence about violence may misrepresent patriarchal strategies in feudal,
colonial, and post-colonial regimes.

Fanon privileges the analysis of male-on-male violence. He says the
colonizer turns natives into animals, who turn on each other in "blood-
thirsty explosions" (52); the torture of "traitors," the terror of guerrilla
warfare. He argues that "liberation must, and can only, be achieved by
force" (73). Jean-Paul Sartre endorses the idea of force in his preface to
Fanon's analysis: "irrepressible violence. . . . is man recreating himself"
(21). Fanon implies a stage theory of violence like a boomerang striking
those who initiated the process. He did not develop the idea that stages
could involve other targets than the boomerang's, such as interpersonal
violence, male against female. Following Fanon's premise, I would argue
that colonialism and neocolonialism in Mexico exacerbate vulnerable
men's violence against women.

Fanon seems to refute his own analysis in one of the most fascinating
if not bizarre chapters of *Wretched of the Earth*, "Colonial War and Mental
Disorders." Using his psychiatric training and hospital work, Fanon puts
violence and its aftermath in the context of public and behavioral health.
Likewise, late-twentieth-century discourse puts interpersonal and domestic violence into the realm of health and behavioral health (or lack
of it). Mexico's violent abusers are what Fanon might call "mentally dis-
turbed" but what legal systems call "criminal." [2]

Fanon's psychiatric cases undermine much of what he earlier analyzed about the cathartic qualities of violence in perpetrators, for he found that it led to lingering depression. His choices and interpretations also reveal deep masculine biases. Among ten individual cases, all but one of them are men. Permit me to lift a case for further analysis (as feminists have done with Freud's case of Dora). This case involves "impotence in an Algerian following the rape of his wife" (254). After French soldiers brutally raped the wife, she "confessed her dishonor to him" and offered to leave him for the dishonor. Fanon analyzed "*his dignity* as an injured husband" (257, my emphasis). The husband suffered insomnia and sexual impotency; he felt guilty because her loyalty (she refused to reveal his location or that of his organization) may have aggravated her torture and rape. The patient said, "If they'd tortured her or knocked out all her teeth or broken an arm I wouldn't have minded. But that thing—how can you forget a thing like that? And why did she have to tell me about it all?" (258). From feminist perspectives, readers can only wonder and ask: What about treatment for the wife? What about *her dignity*? Fanon addresses neither of these issues. But Fanon does provide insight on male rage, resentment, powerlessness, and the way that control of female sexuality is crucial to maintaining masculine identity. Mexico's northern border and its neocolonial economy render many residents powerless and potentially enraged, striking out against those whom they seek to or cannot control: women.

Hannah Arendt analyzes power relations in her classic work, *On Violence* (1959). The era about which she writes is a dying colonial post–European Holocaust world. She raises concerns about strident U.S. New Left and Black Power movements and their vocal justification to fight violence with violence (recall Fanon's justifications). Despite a sweeping title like *On Violence*, Arendt privileges state violence and neglects the social base: families and interpersonal violence. Yet her insights on power relations can and should be extended to gender power struggles, such as women's participation in the labor force, earnings, and male backlash in Juárez.

Arendt defines violence as efforts to multiply strength with instruments, tools that can substitute for natural strength (46, 53). She critiques the use of violence by the state and collective movements; Fanon is the target of some criticism (14), as are Sartre and Bertrand de Jouvenel. Arendt (36) quotes from Jouvenel's *Power: The Natural History of Its Growth* (1949) that "a man feels himself more of a man when he is imposing himself and making others the instruments of his will," and doing so gives a man "incomparable pleasure."

While Arendt has little to say about interpersonal violence, her definitions and clarifications are useful and applicable, as is her criticism of violence as an attempted substitute for power and authority. She writes, "Violence can always destroy power; out of the barrel of a gun grows the most effective command, resulting in the most instant and perfect obedience. What never can grow out of it is power" (53). Northern Mexico's violent gender struggles, I interpret from Arendt, are efforts to command obedience but not substitutes for diminishing male power and authority. What sort of man resorts to violence? Arendt notes that "impotence breeds violence" but that violence as an attempted substitute for power is self-defeating (54).

Like gender analysts, for whom relationality is crucial, power is relational for Arendt. She summarizes this succinctly in the final sentence of her book:

> [W]e know, or should know, that every decrease in power is an open invitation to violence—if only because those who hold power and feel it slipping from their hands, be they the government or be they the governed, have always found it difficult to resist the temptation to substitute violence for it. (87)

I incorporate Fanon's and Arendt's concepts for their applicability to Juárez. Some men, for whom power and authority have slipped in absolute terms and in relation to women and their growing power, adopt violence against women as a control strategy. My next analytic step sets gender power relations in concrete context, focusing on men's losses and women's gains in Juárez: the global industrial marketplace at Mexico's northern frontier.

BACKLASH AT THE GLOBAL-LOCAL BORDER

Mexico's industrialization began well over a century ago, but the process quickened at its northern frontier in the 1960s. The Border Industrialization Program, along with changes in U.S. Customs policies on tariff for value added, facilitated the use of low-cost labor in assembly-line production. BIP might be viewed as a type of pilot test for free-trade policies, with Mexico's entry into GATT in 1986 and NAFTA in 1994. I believe that this context resembles Fanon-style neocolonialism, in which men's loss of control has consequences in terms of violence against women.

Since the earliest foreign-owned export-processing factories in Juárez, people from many walks of life have speculated on new gender dynamics in the city. Through the 1980s, the maquiladora workforce was overwhelmingly female (Fernández-Kelly 1983). Women, mostly very young women, earned money and spent money, nudging at a gender system of men as household breadwinners exercising authority in the home. Resentment in many walks of life built up in Juárez, fostered by widespread media coverage and public unease of women as assertive, productive, and sexualized workers displacing men workers, as Leslie Salzinger examines in great detail (2003). Media portrayals of women created a climate that seemed to justify hostility and aggression. Indeed, early reports of femicide were met with accounts that made it seem as though the murder victims deserved their fate (Rojas Blanco 2005, 2006).

Most women are hardly economically independent and autonomous, given the paltry wages in export-processing factories. Assembly-line workers are paid one to two times Mexico's minimum wages, the equivalent of US$4–8 daily, totaling less than US$50 weekly. Wages have not kept up with the cost of living. In fact, peso devaluations and inflation have meant that workers earn less in dollar terms now than they did a decade ago (Staudt and Vera 2006). Many households send two or more adults into the workforce and still barely get by. But even low wages give women more economic leverage than no wages at all, as research from Mexico City shows (Benería and Roldán 1986), and this leverage threatens certain men's sense of control.

Little research is available on women's wages and household power dynamics at the border. What exists, from a generation ago, perhaps exaggerates more "traditional" norms. Norma Iglesias Prieto describes, from her in-depth interviews with ten Tijuana maquila workers during the 1970s, the naturalized ideology of women who "have grown up assimilating cultural standards of submission, self-denial, and resignation" (1997, 33). Women who continue working after getting married challenge the once-sacred household division of labor because they cannot tend husbands and children in once-idealized ways. Among Igelsias's ten key informants were women who "asked husbands for permission" to find jobs. Just one woman reported beatings, but perhaps others subordinated themselves to the control of men who tested their obedience with intimidating verbal and psychological violence, the early stages of spiraling interpersonal violence.

In Juárez, since the birth of maquiladoras, hundreds of thousands of women have worked formally for wages. Although wages are meager and many women work out of need rather than choice, they do earn and control money. Women's work outside the home has no doubt changed women workers and perceptions of workers. Evidence shows that women in Juárez overwhelmingly denounce violence rather than accept it in self-resignation.

Men's relationships with women have changed as well, evoking a wide range of responses: threat, support, hostility. Men exhibit diversity as a group, just as do women, with at least a quarter physically violent and far more, verbally abusive. For some men, perhaps male rage against cheapened wages under the global economic regime produces backlash and revenge, but they exercise that rage against an easier target than the global political-economic octopus: their partners. Work, money, and new relationships make women less likely to accept the naturalized ideology of female subservience.

After the move toward free-market conservatism in the 1980s, present both in Mexico and the United States, Susan Faludi wrote a powerful, popularized account, *Backlash* (1991). U.S. women's gains in the 1970s threatened the established status quo and its privileged stakeholders, whose privileges also were being undone in the global economy. Faludi analyzes not only escalating resistance to women's equality but also revenge against women. She identifies groups of men most threatened and most active in backlash activities and connects the backlash to the increase of refuge-seeking women in domestic violence shelters, more than doubling of the rape rate, an increase in sex-related murders amid an overall decline in homicide, and woman-killing by partners (xvii). While Faludi's analysis is compelling, more women likely reported crime and left violent homes once violent acts—heretofore considered normal behavior—became criminalized. Moreover, police departments and nonprofit organizations increasingly responded to victims/survivors with shelter, counseling, and arrests of abusers.

"Backlash" explanations in Ciudad Juárez are commonly heard in popular opinion. Sociologist Henry Selby alludes to such backlash in his foreword to the 1997 English translation of Iglesias Prieto's book on maquila workers. At the time the book was published in Spanish in 1985, Selby says, "Mexican men were viewed as more likely to cause trouble, to go on strike, to agitate for higher wages and better working conditions. This is no longer true; now *men are as harmless as women ever were*" (x, my emphasis). Selby analyzes the workers' frustrations in developing targets and goals against low wages and economic disempowerment: "It is a fight against another octopus, another *'pulpo.'* This time not the official political party or the bureaucracy, but seemingly acephalous transnational corporations" (xi). For some men, their economic struggle has been transformed into a fight against a closer target: their partners.

To understand this reconstructed masculinity, shaped in part by the global context of Juárez, studies on the social construction of gender, particularly of masculinities, provide insights. All too often, violence against women is simplistically dismissed as "cultural," as *machismo*, or as some term implying linguistic objectification of "other."

MASCULINITIES:
FROM CENTRAL MEXICO TO THE BORDER

In the last decade, serious scholarly study has been devoted to the construction of masculinities generally in Mexico City and in Latino cultures in the United States. The need for such research is long overdue, given the tendency to attribute a bundle of contradictory male behaviors to the overused popular terms *macho* and *machismo*. The counterpart for women is known as *marianismo*, in reference to the submissive and self-abnegation of the religious figure Mary. The term is heard less frequently but is addressed in dated scholarly analysis, especially that of Evelyn Stevens (1977). Women's survey responses in the present study hardly bespeak self-abnegation.

Anthropologist Matthew Gutmann has analyzed "what men say and do to be men" (*ser hombre*) in the Santo Domingo area of Mexico City (1996, 12). Gutmann aims to deconstruct hollow clichés about *machismo* through a rich description of everyday life. He observes everyday parental violence to discipline children and writes that "mothers enforce the rules more than fathers, even when it comes to beatings" (201). Gutmann describes men who remembered beatings as children and men in a batterers' group who recalled their mothers forbidding them to cry when they were children (103). Women in Santo Domingo "flaunted stereotypes of the submissive, self-sacrificing, and long-suffering woman—*la mujer sumisa y abnegada*" (92). Reflecting on the backlash argument, a reading of Gutmann might make connections between boys' experiences of harsh parenting and their subsequent resentment against women.

Gutmann takes a whole chapter to analyze male violence in Santo Domingo. He says that "men with histories of violent mistreatment of women and children explain that they too are the products of larger forces . . . men as victimizers and victims" (201). He interprets violent men as feeling that "they are losing control over their wives" (213). Gutmann notes that experts identify an increase in domestic violence. Why?

As women's demands "for greater independence rise, so do levels of wife beating and jealousy" (214). Stanley Brandes, examining Alcoholics Anonymous (AA) groups in Mexico City, reports in Gutmann (2003, 20) that "among working class Mexican men . . . sobriety and the abdication of arbitrary power over spouses might well be considered effeminate." Brandes notices how rare it is "for men to express guilt openly over mistreatment of women. In Alcoholics Anonymous, by contrast, men can abstain from drink and ask women in public for forgiveness without necessarily casting their masculinity in doubt." Whatever debunking these scholars have aimed to do, they reaffirm cultural notions that connect masculinity with control over women.

Mexico's North, in the eyes of its capital city, is sometimes viewed as a place that has lost its cultural soul. The North has its own cultural variations on masculinity, and several anthropologists have researched gender and masculinities in Juárez, using the word *machismo*. Focusing on gender construction in the global factories, Alejandro Lugo identifies "new notions of *machismo* (manliness and masculinity)" in the "public enactment of *huevón* and *barra*" (2000, 73), thereby impugning his masculinity with terms for "lazy," especially in front of women. Salzinger's analysis of Anarchomex (2003), the pseudonym for a factory, illustrates how managers' emasculation of men workers spurred dominating behaviors. Pablo Vila, who also uses the word *machismo*, analyzes its reconstruction at the border as a national identity in opposition to the United States and "bossy American women" (2005, 141). These studies suggest that the constructions of masculinity appear to be heightened, rather than muted, at the U.S.-Mexico border as both an identifier of gender and of national difference. These constructions lend support to global and cultural perspectives in understanding gender power relations that evoke violent backlash.

CONCLUDING REFLECTIONS

We have examined global and cultural perspectives for explanations of violence against women at the border. Considerable thought and research on Mexico point to male control over women as cultural—a myth of origin that seems to legitimize rage and violence against women. Paz and Bartra analyze how these concepts are threaded into national myths and symbols, myths that have assumed hegemonic qualities over time. Researchers do not use the word *machismo* consistently, and related behaviors vary from the center to border periphery.

I have situated Juárez in a neocolonial global economy that heightens vulnerable men's powerlessness and augments, however slightly, women's access to resources. Changes in gender power relations produce selective male backlash as a desperate and flawed strategy to regain power; Arendt's insights are compelling in this respect.

Culture is frequently used as a hook on which to place responsibility for violence against women, although culture constantly changes. Uma Narayan has warned of the danger of analysts crossing borders (1997), attributing women-killing to generic "culture," as women-killing is present in many places.

Global and cultural perspectives operate with synergy to advance understanding of ongoing violence against women at the border. Juárez is a site with a half-century of dramatic changes in the workplace, cross-border movement of people and goods, and media attention to gender struggles. Next I will examine what women in Juárez say about their experiences and strategies to address violence.

Chapter 3

WOMEN SPEAK ABOUT
VIOLENCE AND FEAR:
SURVEYS AND WORKSHOPS

Thus far, I have contextualized the border, framed and documented violence against women in the Americas, and considered gender performance as a conceptual tool for understanding changing power relations between men and women, activism against violence, male backlash, and responses from government. In this chapter I will ground the analysis in contemporary realities among women in Ciudad Juárez, many of whom migrated to the border, where they resided in a seemingly lawless mega-city.

I first highlight major findings from the workshops, survey questions, and scales. Women's posters revealed keen awareness of violence, its multiple causes, and numerous strategies necessary to overcome violence. Women's responses to the scale showed their reluctance to excuse abusers who are drunk or blame women for alleged misbehavior. This awareness is especially pronounced among young, well-educated women under twenty-five. Women live with some fear in their neighborhoods and in their homes, where one in four women reported experiencing partner physical violence. To the extent the sample is representative, when both physical and sexual violence are added, one can infer that nearly 100,000 women in the representative sample age group are survivors of violence. But people can count neither on public institutions for response, safety, or shelter nor on the economy for living-wage jobs should they need to exit dangerous relationships.

I begin with a description of the demographics and sentiments of the representative sample of women. Next I discuss the workshops, covering how women diagnose violence and the solutions they offer. This section also shows women's widespread awareness and denunciation of violence in before-and-after responses to the twelve-question scale embedded in the longer survey. After that I focus on the survivors, including factors that appear to put women at greater risk. The final section examines women workers and their experiences with violence in homes and workplaces. First, however, I outline the design, methods, and cross-border partnership involved in this research.

RESEARCH DESIGN, METHODS, AND COLLABORATION

Let me begin with a brief discussion of the research design, methods, and collaborators. Together with FEMAP in 2004–2005, I developed surveys and *capacitación* workshops with a sample of women. The workshops involved active learning, discussion, and work in smaller groups wherein women prepared informative posters to express their own voices on the problems of and solutions for violence. The surveys reflected a typical quantitative research project that, through a lengthy questionnaire, queried women about their work, lives, and risks; the incidence of different forms of violence; and strategies to deal with violence. We divided the sample into two matched groups: half of the women participated in three workshops, and the other half did not. All the women answered the survey that included a short scale ("pre-test"), the answers for which we anticipated change in before-and-after workshop comparisons. All the women again answered the short set of scale questions ("post-test"), for which we compared possible changes between workshop participants and non-participants.

There are several reasons to explain why I chose FEMAP for collaboration, among the wide range of NGOs in Juárez. FEMAP is probably the largest public service NGO with research capability, spanning thirty years of work in health clinics, hospitals, and more than a thousand *promotoras*, volunteers who work at the grassroots level in neighborhoods across the Municipality of Juárez. I had relationships of trust with FEMAP since the early 1990s in conjunction with their cross-border South-to-North technical assistance for *bancos comunitarios* (community banks, rotating credit societies for women's micro-enterprises). Moreover, FEMAP was not visibly identified with organizing around femicide over the previous ten years, although it serves injured women. I hoped that involvement in this research would give FEMAP data and stakes for more leadership and *promotora* outreach connecting anti-violence work with public health services.

The collaborative project was labor-intensive, requiring committed and experienced professionals from the city. Sociologist Adriana Peña at FEMAP's research arm, SADEC, recruited the basic representative sample of 404 women ages fifteen to thirty-nine. We decided to augment the representative sample with middle-class women and with female stu-

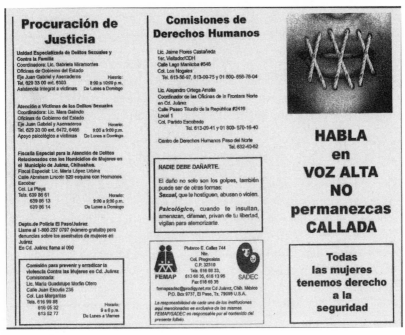

First FEMAP brochure for workshop participants urges them to speak out loud and not stay silent. For the full brochure, see Appendix B.

dents from *preparatorias* (college-prep schools) in order to tap a sample of well-educated young women, especially teenage daughters of middle- and upper-income families in the city. The additional group brought the absolute total survey sample to 615 respondents. In the analysis that follows, I carefully specify the sample about which I am reporting: the representative 404 women, the additional group of 211 women, or the total sample (including both groups) of 615.

Longtime community development activist and FEMAP/SADEC professional Graciela de la Rosa developed the curriculum and ran the three *talleres de capacitación* (capacity-building workshops) in groups of twenty-five to thirty women, small enough for participation and voice. Workshop participants attended three workshops of two hours each, totaling six hours. We developed and provided a brochure to all participants about support available for victims of violence. More detail on the design is found in Appendix 3A. The women in the representative sample came from diverse *colonias* throughout the city. They attended workshops at community sites, often public school classrooms, in the daytime.

SNAPSHOTS OF THE WOMEN:
DEMOGRAPHICS AND SENTIMENTS

Two numeric pictures are painted of women in the representative sample. The first portrays demographic characteristics: income, birthplace, age, education, and marital status. The second picture highlights participants' sentiments of fear and sadness in their places of residence.

Demographic Pictures: Migrants, Struggling Economically

The sample reflects many characteristics of Juarenses: a city of migrants, the majority of them poor, but many with some educational credentials. Table 3.1 shows basic demographic characteristics of the women who comprised the representative sample. First, the women's educational achievements were similar to those of women in the same age group in the 2000 Mexican census: 62 percent of the representative sample had completed *primaria* (six grades) or less, and 38 percent had completed some *secundaria* (seven grades) or more. Second, a majority of the women had migrated to Juárez; only 30 percent were born there, 13 percent elsewhere in the state of Chihuahua, and 57 percent elsewhere in Mexico (mostly north-central states). Third, many women lived with economic scarcity: 64 percent lived within weekly household incomes of 1,000 pesos (approximately US$100) or less, and 36 percent lived in households with more than 1,000 pesos in weekly income. The number of rooms in their homes also indicates economic scarcity: 55 percent lived in one to two rooms, 25 percent in three rooms, and less than 20 percent in larger spaces. Privacy is obviously limited in small living quarters, and conflict may be manifest to all, including children.

Most women are living with partners in marriage (47 percent) or in free unions (37 percent) that are similar to common-law arrangements in the United States. The majority of women presented themselves as housewives (responding affirmatively to the option *se dedica a su casa*—you work in your home), although many of these women may have generated earnings informally. Less than a quarter of the sample claimed formal participation in the workforce, perhaps an undersampled group due to the daytime recruitment and workshops. Almost nine of ten women claimed no organizational affiliation, an indicator of civic capacity. Affiliated women belong to labor unions, which are notoriously weak in Juárez. This question did not tap "social capital," that is, informal rela-

TABLE 3.1. REPRESENTATIVE SAMPLE: BASIC DEMOGRAPHICS (N = 414, AGES 15–39)

Education	*Primaria* (≤6 grades)	62%
	Secundaria (≥7 grades)	38%
Migration	Born in Juárez	30%
	Born elsewhere	70%
Income	<1,000 pesos weekly	64%
	1,000+ pesos weekly	36%
Marital status	Married	47%
	Free union	37%
	Single	16%
Work	Formal, paid	25%
	Household (unpaid) and/or informal	75%
Organization	Formal affiliation	10%
	Informal or no Affiliation	90%

tionships of trust, but for new migrants to the city, social capital is likely to be minimal. Women spoke during the workshops about their longings for greater neighborhood solidarity in a crime-ridden city.

Women's Sentiments: Fears and Sorrows

The survey also allows pictures to be painted of women's sentiments in a mega-city saturated with media attention to very real crime and violence. Respondents were asked whether there was security in their *colonias*, and 51 percent responded affirmatively. When asked the follow-up question about the kind of security in place, most women said police patrols. Such patrols are a mixed blessing, given the mistrust of police and perceptions of their impunity.

Much public attention has focused on the city, its crime, and the femicides, over many years. We asked women about their fearfulness in neighborhoods and streets. As Figure 3.1 shows, more than two-thirds of the women expressed some fear. Everyday life is fearful for the majority of women. Fearfulness cuts across income groups in Juárez (Staudt 2005).

Collaborative research taps multiple minds, hearts, and expertise. Thanks to FEMAP/SADEC's urgings in questionnaire design based on the organizations' previous health research, we included queries about sadness. Less than a quarter responded that they were never sad. A

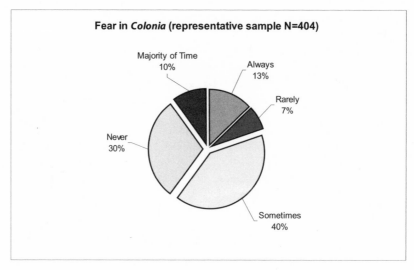

FIGURE 3.1. *Fear in* Colonia

follow-up question asked whether sadness affected their daily activities. To my surprise, almost six out of ten answered affirmatively: 48 percent said yes, and 9 percent added to their "yes" that they preferred not to think about it. We also asked a question about whether women thought about taking their lives in the previous twelve months. Approximately one in ten answered affirmatively. These figures suggest that the combination of economic scarcity and fear may generate debilitating sadness or perhaps borderline depression.

Turning momentarily to the women's words on workshop posters, women gave deeper meaning to these figures. On two posters, analyzed below, women wrote, *No debemos ser mamás tristes* (We shouldn't be sad moms) and *Encontrarle el sentido a la vida* (We must seek the meaning of life). Another workshop poster displayed *Los Caminos* (pathways) to change that included liberty, dignity, dialogue, and *la negación con el llorar y el silencio* (the refusal to cry and be silent). At that workshop, after an older woman said she had spent her entire life "crying and in silence" from abuse, women agreed to end their silence.

These sentiments and demographics permit some understanding of the challenges in women's daily lives. In spite of these circumstances, women manage to raise children, maintain family bonds, and work hard both in paid and unpaid labors in the daunting daily economic realities at the border. The workshops provided space not only for women to talk about violence but also for researchers to assess change in participants' thoughts and strategies, comparing these before and after the sessions. I turn now to the workshops.

TALLERES DE CAPACITACIÓN: TRAINING WORKSHOPS

Graciela de la Rosa designed a fine curriculum, the *programa de estudios*, with themes, objectives, content, and techniques for active learning. Participants introduced themselves and their concerns. They grounded themselves initially through breathing exercises. De la Rosa engaged participants in discussions about violence in homes and the city, and participants listened to music with lyrics on violence. Within the workshops, women formed smaller groups in which they discussed issues further, did "homework" outside the workshop, and subsequently made presentations to the entire group. Some of the posters that women developed became part of the revised brochures (Appendix 3B).

Women's Diagnoses and Solutions

While some subgroups prepared and performed skits, most developed posters that they presented to other workshop participants. The posters illustrate rich dialogue and insights that are worthy of analysis. Many posters show women's awareness of problems, diverse causes, and potential solutions. Women creatively displayed their analyses with their own words, occasionally including newspaper clippings and pictures.

I analyzed forty workshop posters for the substantive themes that women articulated in the workshops. A total of seventy-eight themes emerged. I grouped themes together and categorized them to display the key issues (Figure 3.2), some of which overlap.

In the most common theme, found in one-fifth of the posters, participants vocalized the devaluation of women. Workshop posters identified these typical comments: men's disrespect for women, women disrespecting themselves, women as sex objects, and men's insults. In one subgroup, women pasted a MUSIVI (Centro de Prevención y Atención a Mujeres y Familias en Situaciones de Violencia) sign on their poster with the query: *¿Te insultan, te agreden, te celan o te dicen que no sirves para nada?* (Do they insult you, hurt you, act jealously, or tell you that you are good for nothing?). The women then answered on their poster: *No debo dejarme llevar por lo que me dicen; no debo hacer caso, si no que debo de aceptarme* (I should not go by what they tell me; I should not take them seriously but rather accept myself).

Workshop participants show their poster. (Gabriela Montoya)

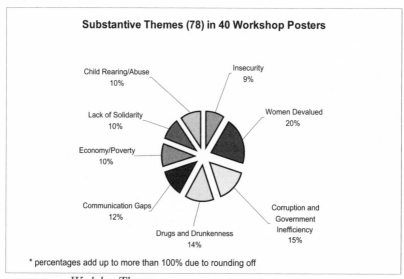

Substantive Themes (78) in 40 Workshop Posters

Child Rearing/Abuse
10%

Insecurity
9%

Lack of Solidarity
10%

Women Devalued
20%

Economy/Poverty
10%

Communication Gaps
12%

Corruption and
Government
Inefficiency
15%

Drugs and Drunkenness
14%

* percentages add up to more than 100% due to rounding off

FIGURE 3.2.   *Workshop Themes*

The second most common poster theme identified gaps in government services, inefficiencies, impunity, and corruption. Not only were women afraid of lawlessness, robbery, and violence, but they also feared the police: 80 percent said they would not report crimes such as physical assault. Yet in a number of posters, women promoted a strategy to denounce violence and crime, including assault, to the authorities and to abusers.

Another common theme was the prevalence of drugs, drinking, alcoholism, and drunkenness. Under these conditions, women said, men abuse women without a sense of responsibility.

Still another important theme involved communication gaps between men and women and between parents and children. Here too, women called for clear denunciations against violence.

The theme of economic poverty emerged in posters. Women cited unemployment, hunger, and inadequate household funds for school expenses, shoes, and the like. Economic issues merged with communication problems on some posters, for partners' arguments often began over economic issues. Poverty, widespread in Juárez, contributes to violence against women.

The lack of solidarity among neighbors was a recurring theme. Women said neighbors should work together and cooperate more.

Women also discussed child-rearing and child abuse as problems needing attention for a more promising future. Two subgroups used elements from posters condemning child abuse that were developed in a MUSIVI campaign and distributed in the city.

Finally, insecurity was identified explicitly as a catch-all category that overlapped with other themes the women named. Insecurity covers sentiments about lawlessness and police inefficiency and/or corruption. The theme reflects social breakdowns connected to drugs, theft, drinking, poverty, and organized crime.

The following list presents a cross-section of selective quotations from the posters. With their own voices, women illustrate the above themes.

- *Que muchas veces no somos escuchadas ni valoradas como mujer, esposa y madre, muchas veces somos para la pareja como un objeto sexual.* (Many times we are neither listened to nor valued as a woman, wife, and mother; many times we are a sexual object to our partner.)
- *Uno de los problemas de la familia es que hay veces en que no hay trabajo y no tienen para atender los gastos de la casa y no tener para comer ni para darle estudio a los niños.* (One of the problems of the family is that sometimes there are no jobs and they [the parents] do not have enough money to pay for the household expenses, food, or the children's school.)

- *Tener mejor cuerpo policiaco para tener más seguridad al salir a la calle y haya menos abusos.*
  (To have a better police department so that there is more security on the streets and so that there is less abuse.)
- *Hay mucha falta de solidaridad. Respetar a los vecinos; solidarizarnos siempre.* (There is a huge lack of solidarity. Respect our neighbors; act in solidarity with them.)
- *[L]as estadísticas sobre consumo de drogas entre jóvenes y adultos se disparan.* (The statistics on drug consumption among youth and adults are rising.)
- *La falta de recursos económicos afecta en que uno no tiene para las necesidades del hijo, y recurre a la violencia, que afecta en los sentimientos de los hijos que dejan el estudio.* (The lack of economic resources affects us in that we do not have enough money to fulfill the child's necessities, and then we resort to violence, which affects our children's feelings and then they drop out of school.)
- *Por lo regular, los funcionarios públicos usan su poder para robar, burlarse, estafar y hasta golpear a la comunidad. Y aunque se oiga feo, hasta violan y matan.* (Public officials usually use their power to rob, trick, ridicule, and even beat the community. And although it sounds bad, they even rape and kill.)

The topic of migration also came up on posters and in discussions, for women mourned the people and places they had left. They challenged the mistreatment migrants encountered in the big city. *Que los emigrantes no deben ser maltratados porque tienen derechos a defenderse y a ser escuchados* (Those who emigrate should not be mistreated because they have the right to defend themselves and to be listened to).

One picture, for me, was unforgettable. A woman drew a picture divided into two sides: *El Campo* and *La Ciudad* (the countryside and the city). The countryside was idyllic, with blue skies, green grass, flowers, and children playing. The city was grim and gray, with no people in it. The woman who drew the picture started crying when explaining how she contrasted Juárez with her hometown.

Awareness of Rights and Abusers' Excuses

In the pre- and post-tests, respondents answered a twelve-item scale about violence, safety, risks, knowledge about counseling centers and rape, and legal literacy. We wanted to see whether workshops might affect women who participated in them compared to women who did not participate in the workshops. As expected, women workshop participants showed some changes compared to non-participants. For the scientifically and numerically minded, six of the twelve questions showed statistically significant changes in the workshop group versus two of the questions in the non-participant comparison group (at the 0.05 level in paired t-tests).

The most important results for me were those from the pre-tests—before the workshops even began—that documented women's awareness of their rights and their reluctance to excuse abusers, at rates of 65 to 95 percent. Table 3.2 lists the scale with pre-test results reported for the entire sample of 615 women, laid out from higher to lower percentages.

As the results make clear, most of the women were knowledgeable about laws and offered no excuses to abusers who were drunk, promised to change, and/or blamed the abuse on women. Reflecting on the myths, symbols, and quasi-Freudian interpretations of Mexican women as masochists, women's responses in Juárez do not bear out those meanings. These women, far from self-abnegating, recognized violence and rape as criminal behavior.

After the workshops, women participants responded with higher levels of information than before the workshops. Five items on the scale showed sizable gains, ranging from 8 to 27 percent, in the workshop group:

- knowledge of organizations addressing violence (53 to 80 percent)
- laws on violence (77 percent to 90 percent)
- not acquiescing to kidnapping/rape (64 percent to 77 percent)
- elbow defense (64 percent to 72 percent)
- wariness about drugs slipped into drinks (61 percent to 69 percent), as the semi-paralyzing, tasteless drug Rohypnol was cheap and widely available in Juárez

Three of these five gains measured as statistically significant, at the 0.05 level: affiliation with organizations, laws on violence, and drugs in drinks.

Answers to three more questions showed statistically significant increases in knowledge and/or awareness: on filing complaints with prosecutors (accurate response); on women deserving punishment (disagreement); and on boyfriends' likeliness to change (disagreement).

From these results, we concluded that workshops were effective but that women began the workshops with considerable awareness about

TABLE 3.2. PRE-TEST FOR TOTAL SAMPLE

Es legal que un hombre castigue a su mujer a golpes.
(It is legal for a man to punish his wife physically.)
Disagree 97%

Si un hombre obliga a una mujer a tener relaciones sexuales a la fuerza es una violación.
(If a man forces sexual intercourse after a woman says no, this is rape.)
Agree 94%

Es lo mismo traer zapatos de tacón que zapatos tenis en una situación que alguien quiera hacerle daño en la calle y ella tenga que correr.
(If a woman is walking on the streets, shoes with heels will do just as well as tennis shoes for escaping someone who intends to harm her.)
Disagree 93%

Cuando algún hombre está borracho y golpea a una mujer en realidad no es su culpa.
(When a man is drunk and hits a woman, he can't be held responsible.)
Disagree 89%

Es probable que los novios que golpean a sus novias puedan cambiar ya que se establece una relación de amor y seguridad.
(Boyfriends who hit their girlfriends are likely to change once they are in a relationship of security and love.)
Disagree 88%

Si una queja es levantada con la policía también tiene que hacerse con el Ministerio Público.
(If a complaint is filed with the police, a statement also must be filed with the Ministerio Público.)
Agree 78%

¿Sabe que existen leyes que protegen a las mujeres víctimas de algún tipo de violencia?
(Do you know that laws exist to protect women from violence?)
Yes 77%

¿Conoce que existen organizaciones y lugares de asesoría que atienden casos de violencia en Ciudad Juárez?
(Do you know that organizations and places in Juarez exist to attend to violence?)
Yes 77%

En caso de alguna amenaza de violación es mejor no hacer nada en lugar de pelear y defenderse.
(If threatened with rape it is better to acquiesce rather than fight.)
Disagree 75%

(continued)

TABLE 3.2 *(continued)*

Si una mujer se comporta inadecuadamente merece ser castigada físicamente.
(A woman who acts improperly deserves to be punished physically.)
Disagree 72%

Es posible distinguir algún tipo de droga cuando ésta se sirvió en alguna bebida.
(It's possible to distinguish a type of drug when it is served in a drink.)
Disagree 66%

En situaciones que hay que defenderse, al cubrirse con el codo o golpear al atacante, puede ayudar a contrarestar algún ataque.
(In case of a serious threat, guarding oneself with one's elbow or hitting the attacker can ward off the attack.)
Agree 66%

---

violence and legal literacy—perhaps more than they would in other cities, given extensive media coverage about femicide. But in workshops, women also had time and space to discuss violence with one another—discussion that had been silenced historically—and they completed workshops with more information and recognition. This is testimony to the value of discussion and workshops.

Young Women: The City's Future

I also decided to separate the younger women in the total sample for their responses in the pre-test scale. This subset of 192 is not a representative sample but rather a group more likely to be higher-income and unmarried. I found that they exhibited even wider awareness of violence and responded with greater denunciations of violence than the total sample as a whole. Consider the following summarized responses in the pre-test: legal to punish wife (100 percent disagreed); drunks not responsible (96 percent disagreed); abusers will change (93 percent disagreed); and forced sex is rape (91 percent agreed).

These results show that even without workshops, young women ages fifteen to twenty-five are aware and knowledgeable in Juárez, a city with saturated media attention to femicide and violence.

Attitudes and Behavior

The attitudes that people express do not necessarily match their behaviors. Surveys rely on self-reports, not on actual observations. Women's extensive denunciation of violence as wrong and illegal might suggest that similarly extensive numbers would not tolerate abuse. However, women's lives, and therefore their behaviors, are more complex than responses on a survey. Respondents do not consistently behave the way their expressed attitudes would suggest.

Once into media frenzy about femicide, from 2001 onward in Juárez, people talked about changing their everyday behavior to avoid violence and/or kidnapping. More parents than usual walked children to school and back home; some husbands walked wives to the buses; some women wore slacks and/or running shoes to facilitate escape. We decided to put a question on the scale with such referents, and the responses illustrated the attitude and behavior connection: optimal shoes for escape (tennis shoes are better-suited than heels). Although rational behavior in an infamous city like Juárez would call for flat shoes, one still sees women in shoes unfit for escape and plenty of shoe stores with spiked heels in their windows. Of course, the same might be said of shoes in unsafe cities anywhere. So on the more serious matter of women rejecting violence, yet for the quarter of them living with it, we need to understand more about the attitude-behavior discrepancy—that is, their circumstances, resources, and self-values.

VICTIMS: SURVIVORS FOR NOW

While women experience many types of abuse including verbal and psychological, the focus of this research is on physical and sexual violence. The overall rate of physical violence with partners is reported, as is the self-reported rape rate for the whole sample. I combined the answers to two questions designed to tap women's experiences with partner physical violence: "Have you ever been hit by a partner?" and "Have you ever been hit by a partner during a discussion?" A total of 139 in the entire sample of 615 answered affirmatively—a large, critical mass of women who have been exposed to physical violence.

Women with Partners

Report rates in other studies focus on women with domestic partners, so I decided to focus on women with partners as well. In the representative sample of 404 women, 341 (84 percent) had partners, and 124 (27 percent) responded affirmatively to questions about whether they had ever experienced physical violence. We asked questions about smaller time units and found that 12 percent had experienced physical violence within the previous year. Of the small percentage without partners, the survey could not answer whether violence had any connection to an avoidance of or exit from partnership, but most non-partnered women were young.

To the extent that these data represent women ages fifteen through thirty-nine in Juárez and assuming a partnered rate of 84 percent, physically abused women in the city would total approximately 73,000, based on the 2000 INEGI census figures (Villalva 2005). These results are huge and serious, not at all trivial. If it takes numbers to dramatize a problem, these figures surely confirm that violence against women is serious. And recall that of the 370 women murdered in Juárez from 1993 to 2003, a minority of them fell victim to the serial-killer crime profile, while the majority did not. Domestic violence, combined with weapons, alcohol and other drugs, and/or non-responsive police, is potentially lethal and has claimed hundreds of lives in Juárez.

Forced Sex

In the representative sample of 404 women, 48 of them (12 percent) reported being forced to have sex. Our question, as it is commonly asked or reported in the United States, refers to completed rather than attempted sexual assaults. Most commonly, for 35 of the victims, the force came from people they knew: boyfriends, partners, or husbands. At one workshop I observed, a woman quietly cried. When others asked why and tried to comfort her, she said she thought sex was always like that. Her case may be unusual, but it is nonetheless tragic.

To the extent that these data are representative of women ages fifteen through thirty-nine, approximately 26,000 women in the city would be rape victims. These results, too, are significant and serious. The numbers are vastly lower of reported rapes, usually two-digit figures annually in Juárez, that is, less than one hundred rapes each year in Mexico's fifth-largest city. Rape is perhaps a more underreported crime than domestic violence, a pattern in the United States as well. Just as with domestic violence, this research documents the seriousness of rape, another type of physical violence against women. Here too, although these forty-eight survey respondents survived rapes, the dramatic numbers they represent suggest a worrisome broader potential for lethal consequences.

Women Stuck in Abusive Relationships

As the responses indicate, many women are aware of violence as a crime. The respondents denounced violence and the excuses abusers offered, from blaming women to drunkenness. Yet more women appear to stay in abusive relationships than might be expected from the attitudes they expressed.

I know of no studies in Mexico about how many beatings, on average, women experience before they flee from abuse. Studies in the United States that anti-violence advocates report in training programs indicate that women endure seven to ten incidents (except murder, of course), thereby exposing themselves to danger.

What might be behind women's reasons to leave, delay reporting violence, or cry for help? Although questions like these are best addressed with qualitative, in-depth research, the data show that most survivors were migrants, fearful, and lacking economic resources to exit unsafe relationships.

Juárez is a city of migrants where the majority live in poverty, comparable to the percentage of abused women in the representative sample. Migrants to Juárez are less likely to have support from family or friends to make a transition. People live in precarious economic circumstances and lack assets to exit relationships, to become self-sustaining economically, and to care for their children on their own. Very little public investment has been made in battered women's shelters, despite the great need.

Comparing abused women with non-abused women, what differentiates the groups most is the battery of verbal and psychological abuses to which survivors are subjected, which undermines their self-value. Contrast the 139 survivors of physical violence with the whole sample: 75 percent said their partners made them do things they did not want to do (versus 25 percent); 70 percent said their partners used verbal abuse (versus 40 percent); and 79 percent said their partners were often angry (versus 61 percent). For women subject to high rates of psychological and verbal abuse, the wherewithal to exit dangerous relationships is likely undermined.

Survivors' Strategies

A series of questions was asked to tap women's strategies in response to violence. Consider survivors' responses in Table 3.3 to the series of strat-

TABLE 3.3. VICTIMS/SURVIVORS' RESPONSES TO VIOLENCE

Never return the attack	32%
Never initiate aggression later	52%
Never accept an attack calmly	46%
Never leave home temporarily	82%
Never terminate the relationship	71%
Never tell others	46%
Never shame by telling others he knows	97%
Never denounce officially	81%
Never seek help counseling help	93%
Never seek help from parents or friends	67%

egy questions and note the variety: endurance, aggression, and passive-aggressive responses.

Few survivors acted affirmatively to denounce violence, whether telling acquaintances or authorities: half to two-thirds suffered in silence. Only one-fifth of victims brought abuse to the attention of authorities or sought counseling and other help at shelters.

In a separate part of the survey, we asked whether women trusted the police to respond to cases and demands relating to rape and violence against women. (*¿Tienes confianza en que la policía atiende los casos y demandas de violación o agresión en contra de las mujeres?*) Mistrust of police cut across educational and income levels: 74 percent of the representative sample and 70 percent of the total sample said they did not trust the police.

Survivors controlled little in their lives, perhaps explaining why they stayed in self-reported violent relationships. Like many Juarenses, most had scarce economic resources; they were fearful in their neighborhoods and on the streets. This fear extended to the police. Many were migrants, living at a distance from extended family and friendship support networks. In silence, they were isolated from those who might assist—whether family members or counselors. Some fought back in verbal or physical form. The verbal and other psychological abuses they endured wore down their self-value. I now add employment factors to the analysis.

EMPLOYMENT AND VIOLENCE

Paid work is an important experience in women's lives, removing them from the potential isolation of households, providing them with resources, and building extra-familial social relationships. I wondered whether women's work had a connection to the experience of violence, not only in the home but also in the workplace.

It is important to remember the meager wages most women earn in Juárez: the official minimum wage of approximately US$25 weekly is hardly enough to sustain a household. While Mexican law requires slightly higher minimum wages in northern states, the difference is miniscule, a few cents daily. Maquila wages usually amount to the equivalent of two minimum wages, or US$50 weekly. I also documented this in the 1990s in research on informal economies at the border before the devaluation of the peso and continued cheapening of wages: maquila workers earned one to two minimum wages, while women informal workers who crossed the border (involving risks and time) earned three times the minimum wage (Staudt 1998). Recall that two-thirds of the representative sample in this research lived in households with total combined earnings up to four minimum wages (less than US$100 weekly).

Competing Theories on Work and Violence

What might previous research predict about the effects of paid work on household violence? The household is an economic unit consisting of people with different access to power and authority. There are competing theories, and the data from this research allowed me to test two hypotheses.

One body of knowledge suggests that women's paid work offers them leverage in household relations, given the mutual dependency and respect incurred. Lourdes Benería and Martha Roldán (1986) examined this relationship in their research in Mexico City with a sample of 140 low-income women. They found that the critical tipping point for women's leverage came when women contributed 40 percent or more of total household income. At this level, women could exit relationships.[1]

An alternative body of knowledge suggests that women's work and control over income threaten men, especially men lacking sufficient economic resources and control over their own lives and unable to fulfill the traditional male breadwinner role. This approach is compatible with the male backlash analysis. Women with money gain some autonomy and choice, for they are not totally dependent on men. Yet work in the export-processing factories has its drawbacks. There, industrial production is rigid and disciplined, unlike the more common flexibility from informal income generation, albeit with mixed and unstable earnings.

In industrial production, women's absence from the home for nearly ten hours daily including transportation time reduces the time available to serve husbands and children: perhaps this absence reminds men about breadwinner ideologies and fuels their anger over perceived gender roles.

One recent study (Carmona, Aguirre, and Burciaga 2005) in a large maquiladora in Juárez with 1,472 women workers—most of them in their twenties with secondary education—cites alarmingly high rates of physical violence: 52 percent of women workers had experienced it, 9.4 percent frequently or constantly. Such results suggest that women workers are at high risk for physical violence from partners.

When the Border Industrialization Program began in the mid-1960s, the factories recruited mostly women—*operadoras*—for a workforce that was 80 percent female. The media demonized and denigrated women workers (Salzinger 2003), perhaps setting the stage for violence and male backlash. As the maquiladora workforce grew and diversified, it became more gender-balanced but retained a female majority. Even under the condition of balance, a current maquila workforce of 200,000 means that at least 100,000 women are employed in an industrial workforce. With forty years of such extensive female participation, the social construction of work and gender has been profoundly altered, with different levels of comfort and threat among women and men.

Women's Work: A Threat to Some Men

In the representative sample, 110 women reported that they worked outside the home. As noted earlier, the daytime scheduling of research resulted in an underrepresentation of formal employees. In the sample, the two most common employment sectors in which women worked were industry (maquilas) and commerce. Women's work rarely produces living-wage jobs, widely believed to be equivalent to three minimum wages (approximately US$75 weekly). Yet work puts economic resources (and influence in how those resources are spent) into women's hands, perhaps freeing them to exit violent relationships. If women know that work and earnings threaten men, perhaps they quit working after they get married or if quitting is otherwise economically feasible.

The analysis shows that women who worked were more likely to report physical violence: 36 percent of working women compared with 26 percent of women who do not work. The majority did not experience physical violence, and thus women did not report the majority of men as abusive. The survey did not offer enough detail to know how many women "dedicated to their homes" (housewives) actually earned money informally, thereby potentially slanting figures. Although the subsample size is small and the difference just 10 percent, warranting caution in generalization, the results support the second approach to understanding the relationship between work and violence: that women's paid work threatens some men.

However threatening, employment produces value: income and potentially self-respect under circumstances of dependency. Women's income likely provides a cushion against the ever-present scarcity of economic resources that leads to conflict. I also wondered if the figures reflected different tendencies among working and nonworking women to even report the painful experience of violence. Working women's exposure to wider social networks, I believe, strengthens their sense of self-value and their greater willingness to acknowledge or denounce violence and to recognize their human rights. I doubt that men's awareness that violence is wrong and illegal or that women have rights has changed as extensively as women's awareness.

I would not conclude from this small subsample that women should avoid work. Family life, valued as it is, likely undergoes great strain with only meager resources to support household members. Moreover, if abused women have no money and depend totally on men, their safety could be compromised from an inability to exit violence and danger.

Workplace Threats of Violence

The survey instrument contained questions about violence at the workplace. Maquiladoras are gendered workplaces that often reproduce male authority and gender stereotyping. However, existing research is based on a small number of case studies rather than the full range of approximately three hundred factories with probable variations in management practices and gender cultures.

The survey questions asked participants about verbal, physical, and sexual violence. Working women reported minimal incidences of such violence, provided in absolute numbers rather than percentages: pressure to date (eight), sexual harassment (fourteen), sexual fondling (seven), verbal humiliation (nine), physically hit (five), and sexual assault (one).

Respondents were asked whether there was a place to report complaints at their workplaces. Thirty-six cited such an office. When asked if they had filed complaints, fourteen responded affirmatively. When asked why they did not file complaints, the single-digit responses included a lack of confidence in the procedure (five women), fear of losing work (one woman), and fear of reprisal (one woman).

Workplace harassment and violence are issues that further complicate women's lives and safety. However, the lower incidence that women report at work compared to the higher incidence in homes suggests that women are comparatively safe at work. Their safety between work and home is another matter, given the city's unsafe public streets. Working women travel to work through potentially unsafe territory day and night. And once they are at home, their risks increase from intimate partners.

CONCLUDING REFLECTIONS

The collaborative research with the representative sample of women demonstrates both a climate of fear in neighborhoods and a reality of domestic violence among significant numbers of women. The majority of women reported no physical violence but lived with fear and unease in their city.

Key results are worth summarizing. Two of three women felt fear from occasionally to always. Among women living with partners, just over one in four experienced physical violence. Physical violence complements other forms of abuse, psychological and verbal, damaging women in various ways. Women at risk for physical violence in the home exhibited characteristics quite common in the city: lower income, less education, and birthplace far from Juárez and from social safety networks of friends and extended family. Fear and sadness cut across income and educational lines. Most victims and survivors of violence did not report assaults.

Women's answers to a scale about violence demonstrated their widespread awareness of the problem and the laws, along with a reluctance to excuse abusers who are drunk or who blame women for alleged misbehavior. This awareness was especially pronounced among young, well-educated women under twenty-five. The results suggest that urban women on Mexico's northern border recognize their human right to live safely, regardless of whether that right is threatened by partners or strangers. Seven of ten women did not trust the police, a sentiment that crossed income and educational lines. In the responses, women criticized government for its ineffective police institutions.

FEMAP delivered a worthwhile set of workshops for women, facilitating active learning, discussion, and small-group projects that produced informative posters, giving voice to women in an otherwise quantitative research project. Participation provided a space to end their silence. The content of women's posters revealed keen awareness of violence, its multiple causes, and the numerous strategies necessary to overcome it. Comparing pre- and post-tests, considerable changes were seen in half of the responses, presumably linked to workshop topics and the brochure about organizations that counsel and shelter survivors. The workshops strengthened women's knowledge about sources of support in dangerous circumstances. As a public health NGO, FEMAP deepened its own awareness of violence against women for its outreach and *promotoras'* work.

Women in Juárez are at significant risk for physical violence, the most foul and desperate cases of which lead to homicide. If results can be roughly extrapolated to the same female age group living with men, 73,000 women in the city have been hurt, perhaps with children watching. Sexual assault augments figures further. Nongovernmental organizations have made valiant attempts to provide counseling and, more recently, meager shelter space, but the potential demand for these services far outweighs the supply of them. The police are feared, neither revered nor sought for assistance with assault. Women employees are at somewhat greater risk for physical violence at home.

Violence against women is an overarching problem, within which a horrible subset includes homicide or femicide. In the next chapter I analyze the pressure applied on government by feminist and human rights activists and later a broader base of political constituencies, including the elite seeking to "cleanse the city's image." However, most of the activism has focused on the horrific femicides possibly committed by strangers rather than on the broader problem of domestic violence. Both are linked, as I emphasize over and over in this book.

APPENDIX 3A: RESEARCH DESIGN

Our collaborative research, conducted in 2004 and 2005, drew 404 women into a sample that matched the indicators in the 2000 census for the female population of Juárez ages fifteen through thirty-nine. Half of the women participated in three two-hour workshops (a "treatment" group, in quasi-experimental research), and half did not participate (a "control" group). Daytime workshops were held in community centers and public schools in various parts of the city. Small children accompanied some of the mothers. In my observation, their presence did not affect the workshop, as most played quietly and behaved well.

With assistance from FEMAP/SADEC staff, women completed a lengthy survey and the scale of pre-test questions that was compared with post-test results for both samples at the close of workshops for the treatment group. We decided on this face-to-face interaction between surveyor and respondent due to varying literacy levels in the representative sample. A copy of this survey is available by email from kstaudt@utep.edu. Women who completed both surveys received a token of appreciation (100-peso coupon—worth US$10—redeemable at grocery stores). We collected more data than the descriptive data and cross-tabulations reported and analyzed in Chapter 3.

We entered survey data when the project was completed, in spring 2005. Once we had slightly surpassed our target of 400 respondents (200 in the treatment group, 200 in the control group), before data were entered, we decided to add some purposive samples, deliberating focusing on female students in three *preparatorias* (advanced college-prep high schools) and on middle-income women. To the base representative sample of 404, we added 211 of these purposively sampled survey respondents, making the final total sample 615. The additional 211 respondents filled out the surveys themselves.

This research design was approved by the human subjects clearance committees at UTEP (Ethics Committee) and FEMAP's Hospital de la Familia (Research Committee) on the condition that a brochure be made available listing locations and contact information for services should women be traumatized by memories that the questions evoked. All women, both in the treatment (workshop) group and in the control (comparison) group, received informative brochures about counseling centers and shelters (Appendix 3B).

APPENDIX 3B: BROCHURES DISTRIBUTED TO PARTICIPANTS

HABLA en VOZ ALTA

NO permanezcas CALLADA

Todas
las mujeres
tenemos derecho
a la
seguridad

NADIE DEBE DAÑARTE.

El daño no solo son los golpes, también puede ser de otras formas:

Sexual, que te hostiguen, abusen o violen.

Psicológico, cuando te insultan, amenazan, difaman, privan de tu libertad, vigilan para atemorizarte.

Todas las
MUJERES
tenemos derecho
a una vida digna,
a la salud,
a la educación
y al trabajo

FEMAP

Plutarco E. Calles 744 Nte.
Col. Progresista
C.P. 32310.
Tels. 616 08 33,
613 60 35, 616 13 96
Fax 616 65 35

SADEC

femapsadec@prodigy.net.mx Cd. Juárez, Chih. México
P.O. Box 9737, El Paso, Tx. 79995 U.S.A.

La responsabilidad de cada una de las instituciones aquí mencionadas es exclusiva de las mismas. FEMAP/SADEC es responsable por el contenido del presente folleto.

Procuración de Justicia

Unidad Especializada de Delitos Sexuales y Contra la Familia
Coordinadora: Lic. Gabriela Miramontes
Oficinas de Gobierno del Estado
Eje Juan Gabriel y Aserraderos
Tel. 629 33 00 ext. 6303
Asistencia Integral a víctimas
Horario:
8:00 a 10:00 p.m.
De Lunes a Domingo

Atención a Victimas de los Delitos Sexuales
Coordinadora: Lic. Mara Galindo
Oficinas de Gobierno del Estado
Eje Juan Gabriel y Aserraderos
Tel. 629 33 00 ext. 6472, 6466
Apoyo psicológico a víctimas
Horario:
9:00 a 9:00 p.m.
De Lunes a Domingo

Fiscalía Especial para la Atención de Delitos Relacionados con los Homicidios de Mujeres en el Municipio de Juárez, Chihuahua.
Fiscal Especial: Lic. María López Urbina
Calle Abraham Lincoln 820 esquina con Hermanos Escobar
Col. La Playa
Tels. 639 86 61
639 86 13
639 86 14
Horario:
9:00 a 9:00 p.m.
De Lunes a Domingo

Depto.de Policía El Paso/Juárez
Llame al 1-800 237 0797 (número gratuito) para denuncias sobre los asesinatos de mujeres en Juárez
En Cd. Juárez llama al 060

Comisión para prevenir y erradicar la violencia Contra las Mujeres en Cd. Juárez
Comisionada:
Lic. María Guadalupe Morfín Otero
Calle Rivas Guillén y Av. Lerdo s/n
Edificio Garita Reforma
Tel. 632 35 56
Horario:
9 a 6 p.m.
De Lunes a Viernes

Próximamente nuevo domicilio
Juan Escutia 235 Col. Las Margaritas

Vivir sin violencia es el respeto a:

- Tu vida
- Tu integridad física, psíquica y moral.
- Tu Libertad y seguridad personal
- Tu dignidad
- Que no seas torturada
- Que se proteja a tu familia
- Que tengas igualdad de protección ante la ley.
- Que se te faciliten los trámites para denunciar la violencia.

¿QUE ES LA AGRESIÓN?

Cualquier acto de violencia que dañe o haga sufrir física, sexual o psicológicamente a la mujer, incluyendo amenazas, coerción o privación ilegal de la libertad, tanto en la vida pública como privada.

Directorio de Centros de Apoyo para las mujeres víctimas de la violencia

Centros de Apoyo

Centros de apoyo psicológico, médico y legal a las víctimas de violencia sexual y doméstica

Casa Amiga
Centro de Crisis, A. C.
Directora: Esther Chávez Cano
Perú Norte 878, Tel/Fax: 615 41 23
Tel. directo: 615 41 43
tel servicio 24 hrs. 615 38 50
Apoyo psicológico, médico y legal.
Horario: Lunes a Viernes de 9 A 5 p.m.
Sábados de 9 a 2 p.m.

Casa MI Esperanza
Centro de Apoyo Familiar en Problemas emocionales
Director General: Dr. Fernando Ornelas
Juan de la Barrera 1763 Col. Melchor Ocampo
Tel: 611 79 16
Apoyo médico, legal y Consejería
Horario: Lunes y Miércoles de 9 a 6 p.m.
Martes y Jueves 2 a 7 p.m.
Viernes de 9 a 2 p.m.

Contigo
Centro de Desarrollo Familiar
Directora: Lic. Sylvia Domínguez
Hnos. Escobar 6150-4, Parque Ind. Omega
Tel: 627 12 07
Desarrollo de Talleres y Psicoterapia de grupo
Horario: Lunes a Viernes 9 a 7 p.m.
Sábados 9 a 3 p.m.

MUSIVI
Centro de Prevención y Atención a Mujeres y Familias en Situación de Violencia
Director: Lic. Rene Javier Soto Cavazos
Ave. Triunfo de la República 3530
UACJ y Gobierno del Estado
Tels. 616 87 13, 616 78 36
01800-SEGURAS 01800- 7348727
Asistencia jurídica y social Horario: 24 horas

Instituto Chihuahuense de la Mujer
Directora Lic. Victoria Caraveo
Ave. 16 de Septiembre y Guatemala #1220
Asesoría legal y psicológica
Tel. 637 56 85 629 33 00 ext 5242
Horario: Lunes a Viernes 8 a 3 p.m.

Albergues

En estos albergues la mujer víctima de la violencia, puede irse a vivir en los períodos establecidos por los centros.

Casa de la Peregrina
Directora: Kathy Revtyak
Quintana Roo e Ignacio de la Peña No. 253
Tel: 615 58 03
Brindan asistencia a las mujeres víctimas de violencia doméstica.
Horario: Lunes a Viernes 6 a 10pm
Sábados y Domingos 7 a 10pm

Centro de Protección de Mujer a Mujer
Directora General: Angela Fierro Sandoval
Calle Tomochic 1455, Col. Manuel Valdez
Tel. 647 17 92, tel/fax 171 7005
Albergue para mujeres violentadas
Tiempo de estancia: 1 mes
Horario: 24 horas
Lunes a Domingo

Vino, Trigo y Aceite
Responsale: Hermana Guadalupe Paez
Albergue para mujeres con hijos menores de 6 años
Cerro del Cubilete 4660, Col. La Cuesta
Tel.: 610 82 72
Horario: 24 horas
Lunes a Domingo

Procuración de Justicia

NIVEL FEDERAL

Comisión para prevenir y erradicar la violencia Contra las Mujeres en Cd. Juárez
Comisionada:
Lic. María Guadalupe Morfin Otero
Calle Juan Escutia 235   Horario:
Col. Las Margaritas   de 9 a 9 p.m.
Tels. 686 23 00 al 09   de Lunes a Domingo

Fiscalía Especial para la Atencion de Delitos Relacionados con los Homicidios de Mujeres en el Municipio de Juárez, Chihuahua.
Fiscal Especial Lic. María López Urbina
Calle Abraham Lincoln 820   Horario:
esq. Hermanos Escobar   Lunes a Viernes
Fracc. La Playa   de 8:00 a 10:00 p.m.
Tels. 639 86 58 al 61   Sábados y Domingos
    de 9 a 9 p.m.

NIVEL ESTATAL

Unidad Especializada de Delitos Sexuales y Contra la Familia
Coordinadora: Lic. Gabriela Miramontes   Horario:
Oficinas de Gobierno del Estado   8:00 a 11:00 p.m.
Eje Juan Gabriel y Aserraderos   De Lunes a Viernes
Tel. 629 33 00 ext. 5 6303   Sábados y Domingos
    de 9 a 9 p.m.

Atención a Víctimas
Coordinadora: Lic. Mara Galindo López
Oficinas de Gobierno del Estado
Eje Juan Gabriel y Aserraderos   Horario:
Tel. 629 33 00 exts. 5 6472, 5 6466   8 a 11 p.m.
Apoyo psicológico a víctimas   De Lunes a Domingo

Fiscalía Mixta para la Atención de los Homicidios de Mujeres en Cd.Juárez
Fiscal: Lic. Claudia Cony Velarde Carrillo
Oficinas de Gobierno del Estado
Eje Juan Gabriel y Aserraderos
Tels. 629 33 00 ext. 5 6275 y 5 6276

JUÁREZ-EL PASO

Depto.de Policía El Paso/Juárez
Llame al 1-800 237 0797
(número gratuito)
para denuncias sobre los asesinatos de mujeres en Juárez.
En Cd. Juárez llama al 060

NADIE DEBE DAÑARTE.

El daño no solo son los golpes, también puede ser de otras formas:
Sexual: hostigamiento, abuso o violación.

Psicológico: insultos, amenazas, difamación, privación de la libertad, vigilancia para atemorizar.

Comisiones de Derechos Humanos

Comision Nacional de Derechos Humanos
Lic. Alejandro Ortega Arratia
Coordinador de las Oficinas de la Frontera Norte en Cd. Juárez
Calle Paseo Triunfo de la República #2416
Col. Partido Escobedo
    Tel. 639-09-42 y 639-09-43

Comisión Estatal de Derechos Humanos
Lic. Jaime Flores Castañeda. Visitador
Calle Lago Manitoba #546
Col. Los Lagos
Tel. 613-56-97, 613-09-75
y 01 900- 658-76-04

Centro de Derechos Humanos Paso del Norte A. C.
Calle General Santos Ortiz # 608
Fraccionamiento Oasis Revolucion
Tel. 1 70 42 03
correo electronico:
cdhpasodelnorte@hotmail.com
Horario 10 a 4 p.m.

Plutarco E. Calles 744 Nte.
Col. Progresista C.P. 32310
Tels. 616 08 33, 613 60 35, 616 13 96 Fax 616 65 35
femapsadec@prodigy.net.mx Cd Juárez, Chih. México
P.O. Box 9737, El Paso, Tx. 79995 U.S.A.

FEMAP

La responsabilidad de cada una de las instituciones aquí mencionadas es exclusiva de las mismas. FEMAP/SADEC es responsable por el contenido del presente folleto.

SADEC

Ilustracion elaborada por las participantes del Taller de Mujeres Contra la Violencia en Cd. Juárez

Centros de Apoyo

Centros de apoyo psicológico, médico y legal a las víctimas de violencia sexual y doméstica

Casa Amiga
Centro de Crisis, A. C.
Directora: Esther Chavez Cano
Perú Norte 878, Tel\Fax: 615 41 23
Tel. directo: 615 41 43
tel servicio 24 hrs. 615 38 50
Apoyo psicológico, legal y médico.
Horario: Lunes a Viernes de 9 A 5 p.m.
Sábados de 9 a 2 p.m.

Casa Mi Esperanza
Centro de Apoyo Familiar en Problemas emocionales
Director General: Dr. Fernando Ornelas
Juan de la Barrera 1763
Col. Melchor Ocampo Tel: 611 79 16
Apoyo médico, legal y Consejería
Horario: Lunes y Miércoles de 9 a 6 p.m.
Martes y Jueves 2 a 7 p.m.
Viernes de 9 a 2 p.m.

Contigo
Centro de Desarrollo Familiar A.C.
Directora: Lic. Sylvia Domínguez
Hnos. Escobar 6150-4, Parque Ind. Omega
Tel: 627 12 07
Desarrollo de Talleres y Psicoterapia de grupo
Horario: Lunes a Viernes 10 a 6 p.m.
Sábados 10 a 3 p.m.

MUSIVI
Centro de Prevención y Atención a Mujeres y Familias en Situación de Violencia
Director: Lic. Rene Javier Soto Cavazos
Ave. Triunfo de la República 3530
UACJ y Gobierno del Estado
Tels. 616 87 13, 616 78 36
01800-SEGURAS   01800- 7348727
Asistencia jurídica y social
Horario: 24 horas

Instituto Chihuahuense de la Mujer
Directora: Luisa Fernanda Camberos Revilla
Ave. 16 de Septiembre y Guatemala #1220
Asesoría legal y psicológica
Tel. 680 06 01
Horario: Lunes a Viernes 8 a 3 p.m.

Centro Familiar Proyecto de Vida
Director: Lic. Juan González Ferrer
Calle Armando González Soto #7522
Col. Los Alcaldes
Tel. 681 09 27 Cel. 044 656 6 26 64 31
Asesoría perzonalizada a la pareja
previa Cita
Talleres sobre Familia Viernes y Sabados de 6 a 8 p.m.

Albergues

Aquí la mujer víctima de la violencia, puede vivir en los períodos establecidos por los centros.

Casa de la Peregrina, A.C.
Directora: Kathy Revtyak
Quintana Roo e Ignacio de la Peña No. 253
Tel: 615 58 03
Brindan asistencia a las mujeres víctimas de violencia doméstica.
Horario: Lunes a Viernes 6 a 10pm
Sábados y Domingos 7 a 10pm

Centro de Protección de Mujer a Mujer
Directora General: Angela Fierro Sandoval
Calle Tomochic 1455, Col. Manuel Valdez
Tel. 647 17 92, tel\fax 171 7005
Albergue para mujeres violentadas
Tiempo de estancia: 3 a 6 meses
Horario: 24 horas
Lunes a Domingo

Refugio Esperanza, Dignidad y Vida
Directora General: Lic. Almendra Robles
Peru Norte 878, tel/fax 6 15 41 23
Tel directo 615 41 43
Tel. servicio 24 hors. 6 15 38 50
Albergue para mujeres violentadas y sus hijos menores de 16 años
Tiempo de estancia: 3 meses
Horario 24 horas
Lunes a Domingo.

Vivir sin violencia es el respeto a:

- Tu vida
- Tu integridad física, psíquica y moral.
- Tu Libertad y seguridad personal
- Tu dignidad

- Que no seas torturada
- Que se proteja a tu familia
- Que tengas igualdad de protección ante la ley.
- Que se te faciliten los trámites para denunciar la violencia.

¿QUE ES LA AGRESIÓN?

Cualquier acto de violencia que dañe o haga sufrir física, sexual o psicológicamente a la mujer, incluyendo amenazas, coerción o privación ilegal de la libertad, tanto en la vida pública como privada.

Wooden crosses precariously stand in memory of the eight young women whose bodies were found mutilated in November 2001 in this same cottonfield at the Ejército Nacional and Paseo de la Victoria intersection in Ciudad Juárez. In February 2007, workers started cleaning the field. (Leonel Monroy Jr.)

American film stars join Mexican film actresses during a rally in Ciudad Juárez at Plaza Benito Juárez, where the V-Day 2004 cross-border march ended. (Leonel Monroy Jr.)

"Disappeared. Help Us Find Her," reads one of the signs held by relatives of missing women during the Stop the Femicide March for Justice on December 3, 2005, from Armijo Park in El Paso to the Ciudad Juárez side of Paso del Norte International Bridge. (Leonel Monroy Jr.)

Rally in Ciudad Juárez at Plaza Benito Juárez, where the V-Day 2004 cross-border march ended. (Leonel Monroy Jr.)

Activist Rosa Elena, dressed as the Grim Reaper, and dozens of fellow protesters march from the Plaza Benito Juárez to downtown Ciudad Juárez on November 25, 2000. (Leonel Monroy Jr.)

Tattered poster depicting a young girl crying reads: "In a present [time] of horror, your silence and fear consent to a future of impunity." (Kathleen Staudt)

A Home without Violence *booklet published in 2001 by the Instituto Nacional para la Educación de los Adultos. (National Adult Education Institute)*

Ilustracion elaborada por las participantes del Taller de Mujeres Contra la Violencia en Cd. Juárez

Drawings and words of workshop participants in Ciudad Juárez illustrate problems that contribute to violence against women (left), what women can do—"Value ourselves!!!" (center), and alternatives to violence such as "inner strength" and "communication!" (right).

V-Day 2004 at the Border. (Alexis Garibay)

Chapter 4

FRAMING AND MOBILIZING BORDER ACTIVISM: FROM FEMICIDE TO VIOLENCE AGAINST WOMEN

Women united will not be defeated!

—COMMON CHANT AT ANTI-VIOLENCE BORDER MARCHES

Change the image of police impunity.

—PLAN JUÁREZ 2005

Since the mid-1990s, a tiny network of activists in Ciudad Juárez has fomented a denser cross-border organized movement and eventually a looser transnational movement of people horrified at the city's infamy, femicide, and police impunity. Movement growth and transformation wrought tensions surrounding representations including issue frameworks and spokespersons. In the course of growing networking at the border and beyond, movement activists built a broader base of political support. In so doing, they moved beyond the frame of femicide to embrace the larger issue of stemming violence against women, a move that itself raised tensions.

To deepen femicide frames, activists drew on horrifying testimonies, quasi-religious icons and symbols, documentary film and theater drama, art, music, and performance. Media-fueled spectacles—from solidarity marches to silent vigils—occurred both with discoveries of new bodies found in the desert, streets, and fields and with seasonal regularity revolving around Day of the Dead (November 1, All Saints Day, and November 2, All Souls Day), International Women's Day (March 8), and V-Day (February 14). Activists roused multiple constituencies through various means, and thereby they "performed gender" with vivid performance activist drama that challenged the normalization of violence against women, using a combination of reason, numbers, and emotional and affective discourse. After many years, the business elite responded, through Plan Juárez, with an emphasis on cleansing the city's image more than its dirty institutions.

This chapter returns to institutions as an explanatory perspective and in particular, networks and NGOs in civil society. Social movement frames overlap somewhat as a cultural issue as well, given strategic choices about symbols, words, and meanings.

The U.S.-Mexico border region, historically a place of limited democracy, is populated with inhabitants who share many common interests—friends and relatives, air and water, interdependent economies. It is a region grounded in a metropolitan area with peculiar local politics involving two sovereign countries (Staudt and Coronado 2002, Chapter 2). Seemingly at the margins, far from mainstream capital cities, border people's voices have historically been muted. But border women's voices have been silenced longer within the mainstream of both Mexico and the United States and at both national frontiers. This silence and marginalization changed with anti-violence organizing from the 1990s onward.

I begin with the historic base of women's activism at the border that was once focused on economics but then shifted toward violence once female homicide patterns became clear in the middle 1990s. This leads to analysis of the evolution of the anti-violence movement, beginning with strongly tied, deep, and personal networks at the border fueled by performance activism that expanded the movement through distant, weak, and issue-oriented ties, including the Internet, chilling documentaries about femicide, popular culture, and other art forms. As the movement diversified and peaked, particularly with large V-Day events including *Vagina Monologues* performances in 2004, it embraced the broader theme of violence against women and stimulated renewed activism, broader constituencies for change, and prevention activities. But such movement successes offered little consolation to murder victims' mothers, whose daughters' killers still go free.

BORDER ACTIVISM: HISTORICAL PERSPECTIVES

Over the past three decades, border feminist activists organized around women's work and paltry wages. Women's formal workforce participation rose in the 1960s, although women's earnings from informal, casual, and unregulated work have long been household survival strategies, however less well documented (Staudt 1998). On both sides of the border since the 1970s, NGOs organized around wages and workforce training; professional nonprofit agencies responded to women's health and violence problems with services. Professional nonprofits like FEMAP and El Paso's Center Against Family Violence rarely took on public advocacy or activism until the early twenty-first century. Sonia Alvarez (1998) warns against the professional NGO-ization of women's organizations, arguing that they are not a substitute for active women's movements. Collaboration between professional and movement organizations would strengthen efforts to end violence against women.

In Juárez the Centro de Orientación Obrera (COMO), begun in 1968, developed a full agenda focused on economics, alternative employment to maquiladoras, popular education, and cooperative societies. Founder Guillermina Villalva de Valdés, a tireless advocate for working-class women, built an organization wherein thousands of women acquired global consciousness and skills to move into various occupations (Peña 1997; Staudt 1987; Young 1987). Drama made working conditions visible to wide audiences through Lorraine Gray's film *Global Assembly Line* (1986). With compelling testimony, the camera captured the hours of work necessary to purchase eggs by the unit or milk by the glass, while U.S. business consultants praise women as "damned good workers" and the ex-mayor of Juárez complains that "we can't find maids anymore."

In El Paso, a parallel border organization known as La Mujer Obrera (LMO) since 1981 has focused on working-class women. LMO highlighted subcontracting practices in the garment industry that produced wage delays, closure, and nonpayment for the bulk of its labor force: middle-aged Spanish-speaking women. After successfully strengthening state law, LMO moved on to address massive closures of the garment industry, symbolized in and finalized by NAFTA. As the federal government allocated workforce retraining funds, El Paso became the number one U.S. city for NAFTA-displaced workers and thus recipient of monies for retraining programs that rarely produced living-wage jobs or compensated for job loss. Since 1994, write Romero and Yellen (2004), "24,000 workers in El Paso have been certified as dislocated by NAFTA" (12), and overall, Hispanic women earned 37 percent of Anglo men's incomes in 1999 (16). Violence against women was not raised as an organizational issue in COMO and LMO.

THE EVOLUTION OF ACTIVISM AROUND FEMICIDE

When disturbing trends in women-killing emerged in the early 1990s, academic and middle-class activists began building an evidence base for subsequent dissemination. Mothers of the victims networked and organized to press for police action on locating and stopping the killers. Mostly ignored and with their daughters' reputations impugned, mourning mothers began to share personal stories about their daughters' tragic deaths and their own experiences with the police: sent from office to office; asked for bribes to pursue cases; told that evidence was lost or misplaced; and worse yet, threatened (Coronado and Staudt 2006).

Symbols, slogans, and sharp discourse began to emerge. *Ni una más* became a rallying cry at marches and on signs. "Femicide" became the language of choice to refer to female murders, evoking more emotional response than the word "homicide" (the official label among law enforcement institutions for murder of men or of people generally), suggesting that misogyny drove women-killing and perhaps reminding people of another stark word, "genocide." A quiet public presence that reminded Juarenses of police infamy and impunity popped up on telephone polls, main arterial streets, and walls all over the city: quasi-religious icons of pink and black crucifixes, which ultimately became movement colors. At the international border bridge crossing connecting the two downtowns, a huge wooden crucifix sits in which nails have been driven to symbolize the victims.

Activists published lists of murder victims, organized rallies and protests, and among those with Internet access, used electronic mail in web-based organizing. Victims' mothers' groups had their own names, identities, strategies, and styles: Voces sin Eco, Mujeres de Negro, Nuestras Hijas de Regreso a Casa, Mujeres por Juárez, and others. Clara Rojas (2006) analyzes some of the representational tensions between middle-class spokeswomen and victims' mothers, including questions about the winning and losing groups in fund-raising activities. Early organizing work was local, although activists and victims' mothers sought audiences with state and national officials.

Placing the border at the center, Figure 4.1 illustrates the networking ties in the late 1990s, primarily in Juárez itself but also with activists in the state capital, Chihuahua City (to where femicide also spread), and the national capital, Mexico City. The border is often conceptualized as the periphery, the edge, and the frontier. Here it is the center—the core of analysis.

Some NGOs focused on service and judicial strategies. Esther Chávez Cano, an activist in the feminist March 8/Ocho de Marzo group, collected data on female homicide since 1993 and framed issues with two prongs from the outset: femicide and violence against women. She opened a private, nonprofit counseling center in 1999. Casa Amiga serves hundreds annually and stays open with extensive private fund-raising. Only in 2005 did Casa Amiga open a small shelter for battered women,

Anti-femicide symbols on a major street. (Kathleen Staudt)

the lone shelter of its kind in Mexico's fifth-largest city. Middle-class activists submitted legal complaints to Mexico's Comisión Nacional para los Derechos Humanos (CNDH), the National Commission for Human Rights, on law enforcement neglect, incompetence, and intimidation.

Initially, Mexican officials in the 1990s blamed the victims, who they said "were out at night," "dressed provocatively," and/or "led double lives." Lourdes Portillo captures these comments in her moving documentary, *Senorita Extraviada*, filmed in the late 1990s but available and widely disseminated in English and Spanish from 2001 onward. The border concentration of economic and political power was formidable. As one activist commented, "We have a lot of people here who are like the Taliban. They don't make us wear burqas, but they kill us. It's part of the despotism of the border region" (in Fraser and Jeffrey 2004).

Female murders continued, and officials dismissed them. Clearly, activists needed to widen and strengthen their influence. Local organizational strength could hardly budge a whole international border region,

THE PERIPHERAL CORE
From local to Border, Binational and International Networks
1999

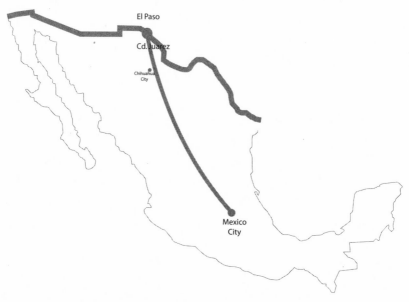

FIGURE 4.1. *The Peripheral Core, 1999*

Wooden crosses precariously stand in memory of the eight young women whose bodies were found mutilated in November 2001 in this same cottonfield at the Ejército Nacional and Paseo de la Victoria intersection in Ciudad Juárez. In February 2007, workers started cleaning the field. (Leonel Monroy Jr.)

shaped as it is with global economic forces and policies emanating from national capital cities.

Cross-Border Networks and Performance Activism: Early Stages

The year 2001 was a turning point in various ways. First and foremost, killers brazenly dumped eight female bodies in the city, yet government authorities did not move. With the close and personal connections among some activists at the U.S.-Mexico border, given its everyday interdependence and border traffic, cross-border networks began to grow: first, Amigos de las Mujeres de Juárez, and next, the Coalition Against Violence Toward Women and Families at the Border, born at a labor conference in 2001 during the annual event to remember violence against women in Latin America, November 25.

Labor activists are acutely aware of the close binational ties that U.S. corporations have to Mexican workers and the Mexican government in using low-cost labor for price-sensitive mass consumption in the United States. The Coalition Against Violence works in solidarity with NGOs to press for systemic and policy changes. It sponsors rallies and marches,

V-Day 2004 at the Border. (Alexis Garibay)

makes presentations at local and distant conferences, encourages letter writing, meets with public representatives (who themselves send letters to the president, secretary of state, FBI, and others), testifies before public bodies and press conferences, and obtains formal resolutions and proclamations from El Paso's city and county governments that occasionally become more than symbols.

Amigos de Mujeres activists worked in solidarity with the victims' families, conducting searches at sites where bodies were found, giving speeches in distant cities, and raising funds to support several groups in Juárez and Chihuahua City. Its informative website (www.amigosdemujeres.org) posts lists of murdered women's names and of news sources. It took the lead in solidarity with the international NGO Women in Black to stage rallies at Mexican consulates, protesting the murders, and later questioning forced confessions and convictions of obvious police scapegoats for the crimes.

Courageous journalists from both sides of the border helped to frame the issue as binational through internationalizing the murder victims. Diana Washington Valdez produced the "Death Stalks the Border" series (2002) and reprinted as a sixteen-page insert to the *El Paso Times* in Spanish and English, outlining the deaths and including the names of several international victims (U.S., Dutch, Honduran). Other journalists and activists, Kent Paterson and Gregory Bloom among them, broadened communication through investigative reporting and the *frontera* electronic news service, reaching a wide range of the public.

Coalition Against Violence border activists attended events with economic stakeholders, giving speeches and asking awkward questions in such venues as luncheons of the Republican Party for the Texas first lady, the Twin Plant Wives' Association, and the Rio Grande Economics Association. At a silent mourning at UTEP, pictures showed hundreds of mourners, with a student dressed as a grim reaper in the center, startling media readers and viewers.

Police departments on both sides of the border have long cooperated over stolen cars. Coalition Against Violence activists used this precedent to ask publicly, over and over, why there was no cooperation over murdered women. The El Paso Police Department established an international tip line in 2003 and responded to occasional requests for training from Juárez. The first such mutual training occurred in 2003 with efforts to secure evidence late one night at the site of a domestic violence homicide. Officers placed tape around the scene and, fortunately, restrained media photographers from moving the body for better shots, for the next morning evidence was found.[1]

Seasonal events became opportune occasions for solidarity marches. As the binational movement was growing, hundreds of people gathered in the plazas of downtown Juárez and El Paso—the Plaza de Armas and San Jacinto Plaza—to march in solidarity, with U.S. activists crossing the border into Mexico. Femicide was more than abstract; it was close and personal, with victims' names and pictures shown at marches and displayed on crosses.

Día de los Muertos/Day of the Dead honors those who have passed away with pictures, mementos, and names on large table or mat displays, sometimes with bright golden flowered pathways to the altar. When activism grew around the murders, family members, students, and activists constructed *ofrendas*, or tributes, with crosses, candles, pictures, sugar skulls, and flowers to remember María, Silvia, and the scores of other sexually assaulted and mutilated homicide victims, many of them teenagers.

Documentary films became an important tool for organizing strategies and raising funds. Lourdes Portillo's film *Señorita Extraviada* (2001) focused on the victims' families, mostly mothers, with respect and dignity, and offered multiple theories for the serial killings: Egyptian

"Disappeared. Help Us Find Her," reads one of the signs held by relatives of missing women during the Stop the Femicide March for Justice on December 3, 2005, from Armijo Park in El Paso to the Ciudad Juárez side of Paso del Norte International Bridge. *(Leonel Monroy Jr.)*

engineer Abdel Sharif, gang members and organized crime, the police themselves, and/or a collusive combination of the above. Victims' families testified about police disinterest and disrespect. The film's opening testimony made it clear that violence against women did not begin in 1993, as Eva Arce, whose daughter was assassinated, testified about her own abduction as a young woman and being sold to gang rapists by a girlfriend for fifteen pesos but fortunately left alive.

Anti-femicide organizing began to penetrate popular culture from films to music and books. Portillo's film was shown widely in Mexico and the United States. For its *POV/Point of View* series, the Public Broadcasting Service (PBS) also brought the documentary into U.S. television viewers' homes. Although the film presents no gratuitous violence or dead bodies, segments stick in viewers' memories. When I approached an El Paso city councilman for assistance in the bureaucratically complex procedures to gain approval for a march and for support with a formal resolution denouncing violence, he remembered the film's discussion of a trophy nipple necklace a man wore: What if that happened to my daughter, my wife, or my mother, he wondered. English-language mystery fiction readers had a field day with many books about border violence against women (Appendix 4A).

Besides film, another part of popular culture is musical performance. In border culture, *corridos* are songs with a message. In *El Narcotraficante* (2004), Edberg analyzes drug traffickers' social-bandit, hypermasculine bravado imagery sung in *narcocorridos*. Los Tigres del Norte, a band with hundreds of hits and big audiences throughout the Americas, brought pointed complexity about femicide to their lyrics. In "Las Mujeres de Juárez," they refer to femicide (my translation): "The bones in the desert demonstrate the stark truth of the untouchable impunity, that the dead women of Juárez are a national shame."

Activists organized against femicide and police impunity, beginning in Juárez, and networked across the border and into popular culture. Binational activists developed close personal ties with border people who share lived experience in the region and common interests in locating potential killers who crossed the border with relative ease. Whether situated north or south of the border, activists initially framed the movement around femicide more than general violence against women, using reason, numbers, emotion, and passion reinforced with personal testimonies, pictures, stories, symbols, and quasi-religious icons. Documentaries, music, and performance widened the visibility of the murders to broad audiences, not simply those who read newspapers but also those who imbibe popular culture. Activists soon set bigger stages that Mexican officials and politicians could not easily contain or co-opt with the typical strategies of minimizing and trivializing the crimes. The foundation was in place for dramatic expansions of a strong movement that peaked in late 2003 and early 2004.

Networks, Movement Frames, and Visibility: 2003–2004

By late 2002, border activists had made femicide widely visible, laying the groundwork for other national and international movements to join and augment efforts. Several universities sponsored lengthy conferences that roused new and geographically distant constituencies. International human rights networks, especially Amnesty International, embraced the femicide issue. Protest rallies occurred in Mexico City, and famous writers like Elena Poniatowska and Alma Guillermoprieto wrote and spoke about femicide. Representatives from international and regional organizations visited the border and criticized it from afar. The Mexico Solidarity Network organized caravans across borders, taking traveling testimonials as far as the northeastern United States and southern Mexico. The Washington Office on Latin America (WOLA), a think-tank and advocacy organization in Washington, D.C., helped organize U.S. congressional visits to the border. Feminists in the Mexican Congress spoke individually and collectively, laying the groundwork to challenge institutions. Nothing epitomized performance activism more, however, than the staging and restaging of Eve Ensler's provocatively titled play, *The Vagina Monologues*, written in 1996. With this production, movement frames multiplied to address sexuality along with violence against women generally and femicide specifically.

In the United States, anti-violence activists broadened the political base with the play. Ensler authorizes volunteers to perform her work without infringing on copyright law "until the violence stops," as the cover of her DVD states. While most monologues portray diverse U.S. women, international monologues illustrate women under conditions of strong patriarchy, misogyny, and war—western Asia and Bosnia, for example. Ensler, based in New York City, promotes the performance of her play to raise awareness about and funds for anti-violence work. For some, the language is shockingly direct, but the intent is for people to verbalize previously unspeakable experiences and body parts with refreshingly direct language. Such language does not always "translate" well across

Three El Paso chambers of commerce host a dinner for congressional visitors at UTEP in October 2003. Foreground center, from left: Representative Hilda Solis (D-California), Coalition Against Violence Co-Chair Irasema Coronado, and the author. (Asha Dane'el)

cultures, languages, and sensitivities including those of mothers still in mourning over their daughters' deaths.

Performances of Ensler's *The Vagina Monologues* occur annually at the border. The event rouses anti-violence activists, raises funds for non-profit organizations that serve women on both sides of the border, and draws participants, especially young women, into the movement. In El Paso alone, community and campus performances drew hundreds initially and in 2004 more than a thousand.

Eve Ensler committed efforts to raise awareness about the femicide in Juárez. She added a monologue on the murders in 2003, visited Juárez for a solidarity rally at the state judicial police office in the city, and participated in honoring Esther Chávez Cano as one of twenty-one international leaders for the twenty-first century. Once distant activists began to align with some organizations rather than others, the context became a greater political minefield. V-Day 2004 events and tensions would grow bigger yet, but I will return to that after I analyze other groundwork and changing contexts.

Movement organizing spread over multiple spaces and loosely tied

THE PERIPHERAL CORE

From local to Border, Binational and International Networks

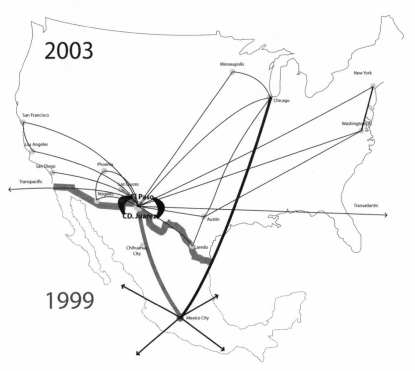

FIGURE 4.2. *The Peripheral Core, 2003*

networks still centered at the border. Figure 4.2 shows the horizontal and geographic spread of the femicide movement. Weakly tied, issue-oriented activists, using electronic communication to air similarities and differences, added new stress to the existing tensions over issue framing, representation, and beneficiaries from fund-raising.

The Mexican government did not stand still while all this went on but used what some might call classic "divide and rule" tactics for which less-than-democratic governments are famous. Governments typically make dramatic gestures to appease movements, co-opt some of their members, and distribute patronage to silence critics. The Mexican government, at federal, state, and local levels, brought activists and selected grieving mothers into its fold through appointments and/or stipends, aggravating the tensions surrounding representation. One outsider-turned-insider was Victoria Caraveo, an anti-violence activist whom Governor Patricio Martínez named to head the Instituto Chihuahuense de la Mujer (ICHIMU), the State of Chihuahua Woman's Institute, with a sizable budget, equivalent to a half-million U.S. dollars. As a spokeswoman for the state government, Caraveo worked with what she called "her mothers" and channeled financial support toward them for counseling and housing. Most activists grew suspicious of her and distanced themselves from her.

Strains developed between border and distant activists, the latter perceived by the former to have their own agendas and particular allies. Speedy communication through e-mail dispersed news of events, resolutions, activities, and opinions instantly. Activists experienced how goodwill could be enhanced just as quickly as ill will through instant e-mail.

Border activists' strong ties got tested as women from distant, weakly tied networks took event-organizing and fund-raising to a whole new level, reaching far more people. While many universities hosted events about the murders, several universities organized full conferences in 2003 with dramatic visuals. Faculty members and students at Arizona State University West organized powerful and moving conferences in 2003 and 2004 titled "Gender, Justice, and the Border." During the conferences, the campus featured hundreds of crosses in a cemetery-like atmosphere with personal words written on decorated dresses for the murdered women and girls. Only the heartless would fail to be affected in viewing the little girls' dresses with angel wings. Three such dresses, auctioned as a fund-raiser for nonprofit organizations, were returned to the border and put on monthlong display at UTEP's library in 2003 and at annual Ni Una Más border youth violence-prevention events.

At the University of California at Los Angeles (UCLA), Alicia Gaspar de Alba organized the Maquiladora Murders conference that more than a thousand people attended. Although scores (rather than hundreds) of femicide victims worked in maquilas, the global economic metaphor has been a powerful symbol to rouse constituencies critical of global neoliberal economics. Tensions had long brewed in Juárez among activists, spokeswomen, and beneficiaries from fund-raising. And over the years, victims' mothers had asked many times: Who profits from our pain? (Gaspar de Alba 2003; Coronado and Staudt 2006; Rojas 2006; Wright 2006). At the UCLA conference, NGO activists, victims' mothers, and ICHIMU appointee Caraveo appeared on stage to exchange their wrenching differences in public. A Los Angeles theater group, Grupo Sinergía, performed a play, "The Women of Juárez," the script for which aligned with one of the NGOs named in the play. The group would later give repeat performances in other parts of the United States, including El Paso during V-Day weekend 2004, when framing tensions heightened over narrower attention to femicide versus the broader anti-violence frame.

Amnesty International had a strong presence at the UCLA conference. Amnesty's posters, in Spanish and English, showed striking visual graphics. One poster shows a road, a cemetery, and a grim sign with the words

Bienvenidos a [Welcome to] Juárez
Habitantes [Population] 1,218,817
MUJERES [Women]

and a large arrow pointing from "MUJERES" toward the cemetery. Away from the border, some would surely wonder how many border women were still alive.

Amnesty International published a substantive, methodical monograph in Spanish and English on the ten years of *Intolerable Killings* (2003). The publication was announced with high visibility and fanfare in Juárez and elsewhere during the October 2003 U.S. congressional visit that WOLA helped arrange. WOLA is another distant NGO that adopted femicide as one of its issues, which deepened its long-term concern with the weak rule of law in Mexico. With its substantial staff expertise in Mexico and Latin America, access to the U.S. Congress, and connections with Amnesty International, WOLA generated reports, press releases, and announcements. All this activity reached even more distant networks and constituencies.

U.S. Congresswoman Hilda Solis, a Democrat from Los Angeles, led the congressional delegation as a response to Juarenses among her "transnational" constituencies who asked why the U.S. government was not doing anything about the femicide. Solis and her colleagues met with officials and activists on both sides of the border. Animosity developed during the delegation's visit as ICHIMU appointee Caraveo and Amnesty activists argued publicly over numbers—¡mentiras! (lies!).

Representative Solis introduced and maneuvered unanimous passage (finally, in 2006) in the U.S. House of Representatives of a resolution to denounce the murders and inadequate governmental response. The resolution not only shamed Mexico but also pressured and educated U.S. politicians. Yet like many congressional resolutions, it offered symbolic rather than substantive leverage, lacking either resources or institutional responsibilities for action. However, the U.S. House is on record as denouncing femicide.

V-Day/Día V 2004: A Peak in the Movement

V-Day, or Día V, 2004 rose to the pinnacle of all cross-border solidarity marches and events. *The Vagina Monologues* was performed in Spanish and in English, and the monologue on femicide put Juárez on a par with misogyny in Japanese soldiers' use of South Korean "comfort women," the war in Iraq, and Serbs' mass rapes in Bosnia. Student activists organized a weeklong conference at UTEP with speakers, panels, and rallies.

Media spectacles had already begun, one of which was a 2003 *Cristina* show on Spanish-language Univision (comparable to *The Oprah Winfrey Show*) throughout the Americas. The show disseminated the names and faces of victims' mothers, evidence, and the surprise identification of bodies.

Media frenzy took hold in early 2004 with the visit of celebrities from Mexico City and Hollywood and the largest-ever cross-border solidarity march in this region, estimated at 5,000 to 8,000 people. Journalists came from around the world, as did activists and newly inspired men and women outraged at the spectacle of femicide at the border. Professional NGOs in health, such as FEMAP, became involved in support activities. V-Day 2004 revealed, more graphically than the earlier tensions, the differences among some border NGOs about whether to broaden the focus to women and violence or to maintain a narrow focus on femicide. Among the movement's internal disagreements, too, was that some victims' mothers took offense at the sexualized, playful vagina-talk in Ensler's popular play.

Dramatic theatrical performances captured audiences that ranged from hundreds to thousands. The Los Angeles theater group performed the evening before V-Day, in solidarity with Nuestras Hijas de Regreso a Casa, named in their play, at La Mujer Obrera's Café Mayapan in El Paso. One group of activists at this event passed word to boycott the V-Day solidarity march and performances of *The Vagina Monologues* over the next two days in Juárez and El Paso. Other border activists circulated at the event, hoping to rebuild or maintain bridges among all those who shared revulsion about violence against women.

American film stars join Mexican film actresses during a rally in Ciudad Juárez at Plaza Benito Juárez, where the V-Day 2004 cross-border march ended. (Leonel Monroy Jr.)

Participants in solidarity march across the El Paso–Juárez downtown bridge, V-Day 2004. (Asha Dane'el)

In Juárez on V-Day, February 14, religious leaders—notably absent in most anti-violence until 2004 except to open and close events with prayer—spoke at the Benito Juárez park near downtown. Maquiladora buses transported activists and visitors to the place where *The Vagina Monologues* was performed. Mexican and U.S. media showed *las famosas*, Hollywood and Mexico City movie stars who also were articulate critics of violence against women and government impunity: Salma Hayek, Jane Fonda, Sally Field, and others.

As the activism reached a crescendo, government unresponsiveness was a deadening, screaming silence. Governor Martínez, still in office, seemingly dug in his heels to resist and ignore activists' demands. One newspaper said to be more closely aligned with state government minimized coverage on Sunday following Saturday's V-Day events, while the other newspaper, a critic of the government, offered far more coverage in terms of space and color pictures.

After the climactic peak, the social movement was in decline, but the issue took hold. In movement terms, V-Day was a tough act to follow. Fatigue and quiescence set in, and the media covered what activists suspected was government-instigated questioning about the distribution of monies, that is, who was benefiting from the suffering of victims' families. Counseling agencies and NGOs require funds to sustain their work (Wright 2006), but some people wondered how much was too much. ICHIMU provided stipends, housing grants, and counseling funds for some mothers but not others, some of whom kept their distance from political movements or perceived cooptation. Questions were raised about who should be eligible for "reparations," or what in Texas is called Crime Victims' Compensation. To activists, the reparations looked more like patronage and pork-barrel politics to quiet critics.

Reminders of Death and Dirty Institutions

An alternative campaign was getting started to redefine the city's image. In Juárez, local television news programs sponsored a series on "foreign" funding and fund-raising drives. Letters published in the local print media, usually a rare occurrence, mounted, with writers expressing concerns about the city's "image." TV Azteca aired a soap opera on the femicide in May 2004 threaded with the reality of words from the official report from federal special investigator Guadalupe Morfín (2004) in running commentary on the bottom of the TV screen. Surely viewers watching the drama of missing and murdered women, at the hands of serial killers, wondered what was real and what was performance. Newspaper columns appeared on Morfín's high salary, rousing suspicion and cynicism. The campaign to paint a better image of the city was well under way.

Peak events, I believe, represented a tipping point in moving the Juárez establishment to do something, if only to invest in public relations efforts to change the city's dastardly image. Over time, activists' cantankerous voices broadened the constituencies for change and mainstreamed activities that deepened awareness of and revulsion toward violence against women in El Paso as well as Juárez.

With the drive to cleanse the city's image under way, few activists wanted to be blamed for the loss of jobs and investment. Since 2001, some plants had closed on the border and reopened in China, and 50,000 Juarenses lost jobs. Distant, loosely connected activists asked border NGOs for contributions to fund a May 2004 Mothers Day full-page ad in print media that would disconnect critiques of the maquilas from the violence. Knowing well the history of activism and the economic factors that lessen victims' ability to get justice, cross-border activists neither contributed nor authorized their names on the ad. The request itself was a poignant reminder that faraway activists lacked details about the region.

After the V-Day crescendo of 2004, fatigue seemed to set in among border activists, at least for high-profile performance activism. Government divide-and-control strategies, perfected over time, eventually took their toll on solidarity. A U.S. feminist organization, late to discover femicide as an issue, organized a cross-border solidarity march in late 2005, but few participated. The films and journalistic and academic writings that followed the dramatic activism were hardly a substitute but still useful for education and prevention.[2] Patricia Ravelo Blancas' long-awaited documentary, *La batalla de las cruces: Una decada de impunidad y violencia contra las mujeres* (The battle of the crosses: A decade of impunity and violence against women), appeared in Spanish with English subtitles. And border journalist Diana Washington Valdez published a book in 2005 that was publicly presented in Mexico, Spain, and the United States, *Cosecha de MUJERES: Safari en el desierto mexicano* (Harvest of women: Journey in the Mexican desert), covering her investigative work (republished in English in 2006). The movie industry jumped on the bandwagon of femicide, releasing *The Virgin of Juárez* (2006). Activists can only wait and wonder how Jennifer López and Antonio Banderas will represent Juárez in the film *Bordertown*. Thanks to Hollywood, dramatic femicide coverage will infuse popular culture.

Social movements create public spectacles and spotlights (Gamson 2005), and border media have responded with coverage throughout. Print and television media relish the coverage of crime stories. Murders and bodies make front-page headlines and lead stories on television. Such stories helped provide evidence for activists who collected names of murdered girls and women and the circumstances surrounding their deaths. The feminist group Ocho de Marzo has collected such information since 1993 and categorized it year by year; it has been reprinted on various websites and in Chávez Cano (2002).

Murder is grisly and painful to read about, regardless of whether strangers, acquaintances, or partners committed the crimes: a dead woman is a dead woman. Consider the following from hundreds of descriptions collected by Ocho de Marzo and reprinted elsewhere, some women and girls named and others unknown (I removed locations and surnames, but see Chávez Cano 2002 and S. García 2005 for names):

[1993] *Caso No. 16. Noviembre 15. Esmeralda . . . 13 años . . . Raptada al salir de la escuela. . . . Violada . . . anal y vaginal. Estrangulada. Su cuerpo se localizó atrás de la escuela.*
[Esmeralda, thirteen years old, raped (anal and vaginal) leaving school, strangled, her body located behind the school.]

[1995] *Caso No. 16. Septiembre 5. Desconocida. 24 años . . . Atada de manos con correa de bolsa de mujer. Desnucada, herida cortante en brazo derecho, amputación de seno derecho y pezón izquierdo amordidas.*
[Unknown, twenty-four years old, tied with the strap of a women's purse. Broken neck, wounds on the right arm, right breast amputated, and left nipple bitten off.]

[1997] *Caso No. 21. Noviembre 30. Teresa . . . 32 años . . . fue asesinada con un cuchillo ayer. . . . aparentemente estaba separada y el esposo tuvo una discusión con ella.*
[Teresa, thirty-two years old, killed with a knife yesterday . . . apparently was separated and the husband had an argument with her.]

[2001] *Caso 6. Febrero 21. El cuerpo de una niña de tres años de edad, de nombre Reina . . . con hematomas en todo su cuerpo y señales de estrangulamiento. . . . la niña fue violada recientemente.*
[The body of a three-year-old girl named Reina . . . with swollen bruises all over her body and signs of strangulation . . . The girl was recently raped.]

The lists reveal the diverse women and girls who died (young, old) along with the diverse methods (knifed, strangled, beaten, burned), killers (known, unknown), and motives (revenge, sadism). The high-volume list shows that murder and violence against women is not only serial-killer attacks by strangers but the sort of routine sexualized torture associated with female homicide found in many cities and countries. The murders continue, and updates like the following (from www.amigosdemujeres .org) are posted on websites.

[2005] Alejandra, thirteen, found in her home raped and beheaded.

[2006] Skeletal remains of a teenaged girl found on the side of the road, disposed of eight months earlier.

Political campaigns generated media coverage, and political party web-sites contained nearly boundless rhetoric with promises. As the Chihua-hua gubernatorial campaign heightened in 2004, activists and candidates interacted little about either femicide or domestic violence (although this had changed by 2006). Many activists expressed profound cynicism about the political establishment, especially in Mexico. But candidates realized the public relations disaster that the city had become.

In Juárez, local council representatives seemed politically impotent, but their counterparts in El Paso could exercise more authority. The ex-pansion from femicide frames to violence against women spurred other anti-violence strategies in El Paso. Next I turn to the analysis of border activists who shifted strategies and targets to renewing awareness of vio-lence against women in their own backyard.

Reinvigorated Work in El Paso

Involved for several years in the high-profile movement against femicide in Juárez, El Pasoans in the Coalition Against Violence mobilized to address a woman-beater on the El Paso City Council in 2005. It acted after firm evidence and documentation emerged through the media about a district court judgment against an incumbent seeking reelection who had been ordered to pay damages for his injuries to a woman thirty years earlier. Fortuitously, the coalition had obtained unanimous sup-port in City Council proclamations denouncing violence against women in 2003 and 2004 (Appendix 4B). The symbolic resolutions became an important activist tool.

The incumbent, Robert Cushing, had not paid the $50,000 damages for hospitalization and dental reconstruction despite the survivor's continuous renewal of judicial orders for compensation. Coalition members followed procedures for adding public comment to open meetings, posting items on the City Council agenda website three days before the meeting: its one-page statement, "No Woman Beaters on City Council," and the City Council's V-Day 2004 proclamation denouncing violence as backup. All this material was included in the council members' agenda packets. The coalition sought the councilman's removal from legislative committees that gave him oversight of the police and of budgetary matters that involved women. Coalition members and supporters attended several council meetings in full force, carrying pink (for femicide) and purple (for domestic violence) flowers to establish their public identity while they waited for their place on the agenda, which the councilman's supporters reorganized to pose delays. Coalition members offered a flower to each City Council member—including the two women members—but only one councilman (later elected mayor) accepted the flower.

In very public, high-visibility media coverage, both print and broadcast, Cushing at first denied the action, then made no comment, and finally apologized for his "indiscretions" during youth. Members of the public wrote letters to the editor of the *El Paso Times* and to a local television news station, both to criticize Cushing and to praise him. A portion of the wider public, probably a minority, did not view woman-beating as a crime. A local news affiliate announcer read several letters from viewers, including one who wondered whether the survivor deserved the beating. This was a stark reminder of the misogyny within local culture.

Turning points came with two media events. First, the survivor, Belinda, who had moved away in fear for her life, returned to El Paso to give a widely covered press conference. Second, media stories resurfaced that the councilman had disemboweled a dog owned by his fiancé, an act for which a police report was filed. For some members of the public, animal abuse was worse than beating a woman. For other members of the public, the disembowelment confirmed a problematic character issue. The incumbent did not win reelection. At the close of 2005, the *El Paso Times* listed this among its top-ten stories of the year. The story produced extensive public education on violence against women, perhaps lowering tolerance levels.

The incident raises questions about the narrow content of candidate disclosure forms. In Texas and the City of El Paso, disclosure forms

focus on money and potential conflicts of interest rather than on police reports, district court judgments, or crimes. Coalition members
articulated the need for broader disclosure requirements to inform the
voting public about serious background issues. New City Council members held a town hall meeting in December 2005 at which I was invited
to make a presentation. My preliminary research, amazingly, uncov-
ered no such ordinances from other cities that could be replicated in
El Paso, for other states and cities also focus mainly on financial conflicts of interest.

The anti-femicide movement born in Juárez stimulated broader networking and organizing on violence against women. Coalition activists
in El Paso used tools available in civil society and political institutions in
their own backyard to confront an adjudicated abuser in charge of public
safety oversight and to educate the public about the scourge of violence
against women. In so doing, the coalition broadened its base of support
from feminists and human rights activists to the general public. Many
such opportunities are available in other communities. There is, I believe, a nearly "silent majority" of people in many communities who have
observed or experienced abuse. In Juárez, a broader base of constituencies outraged about violence against women and femicide emerged, but
their motivations appeared to be more about the city's image than the
problem of violence. To this analysis I now turn.

From Movement to Organized Business: Cleansing the City Image

Grim realities and movement activists aroused the business community
in Juárez. This mega-city depends on local and foreign investments that
flow with perceptions of stability.

When the anti-violence movement peaked in late 2003 and early
2004, city boosters circulated a well-designed but defensive electronic
communication about ten points on the city, *Los 10 Puntos de Juárez.*
The message was infused with praise for the city, worry about the down-
turn of maquila investment, and allegations that the women murders
were highly exaggerated compared to crime-ridden cities in the United
States. *Juárez no es la capital del crimen ni TAMPOCO el paraíso del crimen
organizado* (Juárez is neither the crime capital nor a haven for organized
crime). That communication ended with a message calling for a change
in the image of Juárez: *a cambiar la imagen de CIUDAD JUÁREZ.*

Years before, in 1999, public, business, and corporate leaders—

foreign and national—started a nonprofit organization to develop a strategic plan for the city, the Plan Estratégico de Juárez. Drawing on a well-crafted process from Spain, consultants came to initiate partnerships based on diverse voices to imagine and plan the city's future. After massive data collection, Plan Juárez produced a diagnostic document in 2003 and in 2004, "Juárez 2015: The City We Will Become." The well-funded organization reflects cross-border qualities, with memberships that include both Mexican and U.S. business leaders who pay associate memberships that reach US$15,000, according to its website (www .planjuarez.org). Plan Juárez Director Lucinda Vargas formerly worked as an economist at the Dallas office of the U.S. Federal Reserve Bank. Its elaborate website contains information about contributors, amounts, and affiliates in both English and Spanish.

The vision for 2015, with four strategic directions, addresses what the plan calls "base elements." One of them is "the need to drastically reduce crime levels and to end the image of impunity." In Strategic Direction 2, the plan envisions "Juárez [to be] a socially-integrated place with high quality of life." A substrategy advocates plans "against crime, violence and impunity." Impunity had become a code word in both the anti-femicide and pro-democracy movements, referring to police impunity and the necessity of the rule of law. Thus, attention to public safety is threaded throughout the report, drawing on voices from focus groups, surveys, and multiple constituencies. The plan was a hopeful sign that officials would respond to influential civic leaders affiliated with the plan to stop or cut the murder rate (rather than the well-honed tradition of disputing the murder numbers), through reforming the police, investigation, and prosecution institutions and processes.

Would the establishment cleanse the dirty law enforcement institutions or just change the image of the city? Mixed signals have emerged at both the city and state levels. I believe that V-Day in February 2004 and its massive local, national, and international coverage marked a turning point for powerful Juarenses to act on their city's image with the appearance of reforms. Time will tell whether these institutional reforms are real.

By mid-2004, business leaders and their government counterparts publicly espoused the need for action. According to Chamber of Commerce (CANACO) President Juan Salgado Vásquez, quoted in *El Paso Inc.*, a weekly English-language business newspaper, "We depend on foreign investment and tourists as well as foreign maquilas that want to set up in this city. And with the current situation, we are sure this deters them" (González 2004). In the same article, state judicial police spokesman Mauro Conde attributed murders to organized crime but said, "We understand that this increases the bad image of the city." The Chamber of Industry and Transformation (CANACINTRA) president linked concerns to women: "Our daughters walk in the streets, and that worries us a great deal. We want our city back—the big flows of investment that we had . . . and the tourists that cross to walk around downtown."

When President Fox met with six hundred business leaders at the border in September 2004 at the elegant Cibeles conference center, Mexico-born El Paso maquila owner Cecilia Levine ended her speech on an awkward note: the killings of women. Fox responded that he was committed to creating a "culture of legality in Mexico" (Gilot 2004).

In late November, the media prominently covered meetings of the Consejo Coordinador Empresarial (business coordinating council), which developed a new integrated public security plan reportedly approved by eighty organizations in an umbrella civic group (Simental 2004). Urban development officials added that ISO 9001 standards would be used to improve the local governance coordination. ISO technical standards are widely used in the foreign export-processing industry, symbolizing a culture of transnational procedural efficiency. A new procedural crime-prevention initiative is based in Juárez that includes an industrial police program. Some border residents cynically wonder if this is just more symbolic politics or if the political will has finally emerged to establish professional criminal justice institutions that operate with integrity. Ultimately, the border elite will either use its strategic positions and resources to fund real reform, or it will not. Activists have made a dent in motivating those who rule Juárez, even if their motives are self-serving and superficial.

Faith-Based Leaders: Outraged Latecomers

Human rights and feminist movement activists often appear to work in the margins of mainstream public opinion. Although faith-based communities espouse principles that seem compatible with life and safety, they do not necessarily respond to human rights discourse. At the border, religious leaders have been latecomers or absent from the anti-femicide and anti-violence movements, despite activists' use of quasi-religious icons such as crosses and crucifixes to dramatize and legitimize their cause. When clergy speak and write about violence against women, new constituencies become aware and potentially involved, thus reaching beyond the human and women's rights base of the movement.

The border is home to far more Catholics than Protestants. At public anti-femicide rallies, a priest or nun frequently opens and closes activities with prayers. But Catholic institutional attention is focused on immigrants who die crossing the border—numbering hundreds annually (Staudt and Coronado 2002: Chapter 6).

In April 2005, the Presbyterian churches of the United States and Mexico hosted a cross-border solidarity event called "Save the Women," a title with dramatic, though patronizing, appeal. The message emphasized that "we are called" to counter the violence. In the Prayer of Confession, people read: "We confess to you that we have created societies of disposable people, in a world too swift to violence, too prone to fear, too short on compassion. Then, when the suffering of others is too much to bear, we turn away to other distractions." System critiques and binational responsibility are clear in these remarks. Moreover, a cross-border Lutheran initiative in October 2005 called people to the border fence separating the two countries to remember the victims and to act on their faith.

Other faith initiatives have reminded border activists about fundraising in the name of the murdered women and the distribution of monies. After coverage in Juárez newspaper *El Diario*, a California evangelical church initiative also patronizing in its language—"Save Juárez"—raised suspicions, given a website with contradictory information about plans to raise large sums of money. The actions evoked worry that yet another group would profit from the pain.

The evolution of anti-femicide activism shows development, peaks, and spread to wider constituencies on both sides of the border. Activism around femicide and violence against women broadened the base of political support for public safety and law enforcement institutional reforms. Activism began with women and human rights groups, included some labor unions, and tapped religious denominations, health NGOs, and teachers. The business community also was roused in Plan Juárez, at least for the image of the city, since murderers rarely targeted wealthy girls and women.

Performance activism and media attention heightened awareness and fear among all women, generating broad constituencies for change toward professional law enforcement. Activists used fear and symbol-laden drama, but the strategies fell on deaf ears after some years, with the public becoming immune or turning instead to more dramatic and horrifying numbers, which femicide in Guatemala now provides. Second-stage actions are necessary to sustain awareness around violence against women through other means. We next examine the ways that movement concerns have spread into prevention and popular culture awareness among youth, not only the "others" across borders.

FROM MOVEMENTS TO PREVENTION PROGRAMS

Young people are at high risk for experiencing and/or observing family violence, interpersonal violence, and abusive relationships. In the Paso del Norte Health Foundation Youth Risk Survey (2003), 67 percent of boys and 43 percent of girls ages thirteen and fourteen reported involvement in violence; 59 percent of the young teens reported that they had used alcohol, perhaps more accessible to them than to youths in nonborder locales, given the lower drinking age in Mexico and the massive draw that bars hold for El Paso teens, for whom another country is a five-minute walk away. For raising awareness and social change to reduce violence, middle and high school campuses are crucial places to begin constructing solutions.

In El Paso, many families are touched by violence including the murders of men and women in Juárez. At events on campuses and face-to-face encounters, one occasionally hears individuals make comments like, "My cousin disappeared," or "One of my relatives was killed like that." Students talk about experiences with abusive police in Juárez, such as forced sex and the modernization of petty corruption: an escort to the nearest automated teller machine (ATM) to obtain the standard US$20 payment to avoid traffic fines.

Silvia Rede, a teacher at Bowie High School, and I have collaborated around the annual Ni Una Más event since 2003. We hope to spur awareness year-round so high school students will watch out for their friends, report crimes to authorities, and develop new kinds of relationships based not on control and traditional stereotypes but on equal partnership. At the first such event in El Paso, in 2003, the Bowie High School *mariachi* group played the well-known sad song sometimes associated with funerals, "Amor Eterna," to honor and mourn the murdered women in Juárez. This song produced an eerie quiet in the teen audience, punctuated only with sobs. The engaging events involve drama, but it is contained and sustained with follow-up activities to spread awareness about violence.

Teens, male and female, attend these anti-violence prevention events. The day includes a short clip from *Señorita Extraviada* and presentations from the Center Against Family Violence, the Sexual Trauma and Assault Response Service (STARS), the Police Department, and the county and district attorneys' offices. Parents who have lost their daughters to homicide give personal testimonies. One of them was Linda King, whose daughter, armed with a civil remedy—a paper protective order—was murdered by her husband. He subsequently was sentenced to just ten years in prison; people in El Paso's victims' constituency wrote letters to the parole board when he was up for early release after serving only half his sentence. The early release request was denied.

The all-day conference engages students with documentaries, speakers, and the arts, such as interpretive dance, dramatic skits, and poetry. At the outset, interactive discussions with students reveal the already normalized perception of violence and a readiness to blame women and their clothing choices for sexual assault. Speakers call upon students to participate in meaningful activities on their campuses and communities, thus stimulating leadership and active learning. The following list is representative of the range of responses to the question "What are the three most important conclusions you have drawn about violence at the border based on activities and/or speakers in Ni Una Más 2005?":

- To always go in groups and look out for each other.
- You have to be careful who you trust.
- That sexual abuse isn't just about sex.
- You decide who touches your body.
- We can help make a difference in our communities.
- Men and women are equal.
- Violence is about having power.
- We have to unite so that we can make this stop, together.
- Women have to be respected.
- A rape victim is not responsible for the attacker's action.
- Silence is the most powerful weapon for violence.

Some students participate in campus groups with names that illustrate their missions: Lifesavers, Safety Club, Teen Talk, Girl Power, Boys Club, and more. Students suggest ideas that can and should be pursued year-round, such as school newspaper articles and letters to the editor, fund-raisers for battered women's shelters, posters, poetry, essay contests, plays, and skits. Many students have said they would teach others what they learned. One made this comment: "I will not abuse women because I am a man." Students' words are eloquent. After a whole day of powerful and moving speakers, using reason and emotion, one student

Logo for the Center for Civic Engagement Ni Una Más *service-learning program of court observations and high school presentations.*

wrote: "My heart hurts." There is some drama, but its effect is to engage and sustain commitment.

Interpersonal violence touches students' lives at epidemic levels—comparable if not worse than drug and alcohol programs, for which plentiful program resources are available. "People abuse" is on a par with "substance abuse."

At the university level, students participate in service-learning and extracurricular activities that enhance their awareness of strategies to eradicate violence. For example, a Center Against Family Violence partnership, also called Ni Una Más, engages more than fifty UTEP students a semester from various classes for twenty hours each in making presentations about interpersonal violence in high schools and observing protective order hearings and domestic violence trials in county and district courts. The University of Texas at Brownsville has replicated the program in partnership with comparable nonprofit and public agencies.

Students from Juárez also organize activities such as musical concerts. On Latin America Violence Against Women Day (November 25) in 2005, young women musicians put on the "Divas Time" concert. In Las Cruces, New Mexico, thirty miles from the border with Mexico, the Amigos de Mujeres group organizes memorial services to remember murdered women found in the surrounding desert.

Dramatic performance activism has begun to reduce the toleration of violence against women. Follow-up activities occur in schools and higher education, but continuous and sustained prevention activities are needed to undermine a still-strong culture of tolerating violence against women.

CONCLUDING REFLECTIONS

The base of constituencies that address the extensive violence has grown and broadened from an initial focus on femicide to subsequently encompass multiple forms of violence against women. Border activists built a dramatic, personal, symbol-laden, and performance-oriented movement that began with strong personal networks, reached across the border, and eventually involved activists in other parts of the United States and the world.

Dazzling gender performances dramatized women-killing in Juárez in literal and figurative ways. Rallies, marches, testimonials, and plays were performed that led to tension over representation, funds, and strategies. In the process, Juárez appeared to be demonized as the female murder capital of the world, given the serial-killer themes, mutilation murders, and global frontlines for export-processing industrial production. Movement tensions also emerged over the priority given to particular frames: serial-killer femicide versus the everyday normalization of violence against women and domestic homicide. Violence against women and woman-killing have long histories and have become so normalized that they fail to rouse and mobilize constituencies for change. Dramatic activism rouses people but depends heavily on episodic events and the media rather than everyday sustained reform. Yet without the activism, the professional nonprofit advocates retreat into minimal visibility: only to their "clients," funders, and law enforcement institutions.

The murders are poignant, painful, and clear outliers in the normalized violence against women: the prospect of killers hunting for young victims to rape and mutilate before murdering them is a bleak commentary on men's inhumanity to women. But ultimately femicide and other violence against women are linked; understanding this link, activists have broadened and deepened their involvement in prevention, education, and constituency building for change in their own communities.

With a tarnished image of Juárez, the ruling elite and its organized counterparts in Plan Juárez developed strategies for change. Several faith-based communities also realized that movement issues resonated with their principles. What can and will be accomplished in institutional reform? In the next chapter, I analyze and compare institutions for their symbolic or real responses to violence against women.

APPENDIX 4A: FICTION OR NONFICTION?

Over the years, many novels on the border and female murders have entered the popular culture fiction mainstream, contributing to a culture of fear in people's entertainment reading (Glassner 1999). English-language mystery fiction brings the drama of the border to life along with its key symbols: maquiladoras, drugs, and murdered women. One of the first I encountered was Janice Steinberg's *Death Crosses the Border* (1995), situated in the San Diego–Tijuana area and involving women workers, toxic waste disposal in the maquila industry, class privilege, and corrupt politicians. Another maquiladora worker murder plot spurs James C. Mitchell's *Choke Point* (2004), based in Tucson, only seventy miles from the border.

High-profile mystery writers who publish high-volume paperback series embellish readers' imaginations. Take Michael McGarrity, author of forty-four books and recognized in the top-ten crime novel category for 1998–1999. Readers can trace cross-border wrongs in his New Mexico novels with his protagonist, the ethical police investigator Kevin Kerney, solving horrendous crimes against humanity that span the desert and mountains of both the Land of Enchantment (New Mexico) and Chihuahua. In Kerney's novel *The Big Gamble* (2002), vulnerable young women sign up for expensive modeling courses in Albuquerque but get pulled into prostitution rings via drug addictions. In *Serpent's Gate* (1998), based mainly in northern New Mexico, a wealthy Mexican art connoisseur, drug lord, and mall and apartment financier directs an efficient crew of killers who call him *patrón*. He orders the death of a state art director with a voracious sexual appetite, and his crew members dump her body at his ranch in Chihuahua.

The novel most closely tied to femicide is *Desert Blood: The Juárez Murders* (2005), written by El Paso–born Alicia Gaspar de Alba, an English and Chicano studies professor at UCLA, where she organized the Maquiladora Murders conference of 2003. The novel begins with a grisly depiction of a murder in progress of a pregnant maquiladora worker and continues with the abduction of the protagonist's sister. The plot threads together all the competing theories associated with femicide and the depravity of cross-border trafficking rings.

Although *Desert Blood* is a painful read, none quite curdles the soul (and reached more than 700,000 readers, its print run) like J. A. Jance's *Day of the Dead* (2004). The title itself reflects the border post-Halloween celebration of Día de los Muertos, a day of remembrance and of mourning that anti-violence activists adopted with publicly placed altars and shrines to remember the victims. Jance, writer of thirty-two novels, attracts a wide readership for all her fiction, including eleven set in a southern Arizona area adjoining Mexico's state of Sonora. The cross-border ring in *Day of the Dead* involves an orphanage in Sonora that trafficks young women to a U.S. medical doctor for sexual torture.

With a whole genre of novels like these, the image of the border and its demons on both sides—fiction or nonfiction—affects the consciousness of readers. Perhaps the activism, then dramatic performance, and spread into popular culture have made a deeper impression in popular perceptions than business campaigns to clean up the city's image; but fiction's agenda encompasses the entertainment of fear rather than institutional reform.

APPENDIX 4B: V-DAY 2004 PROCLAMATION, CITY OF EL PASO

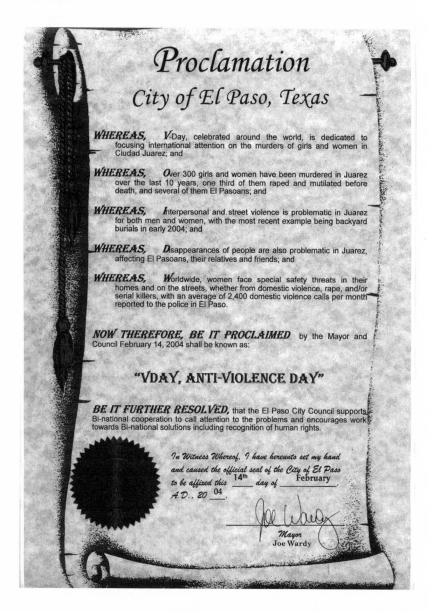

Proclamation
City of El Paso, Texas

WHEREAS, V-Day, celebrated around the world, is dedicated to focusing international attention on the murders of girls and women in Ciudad Juarez; and

WHEREAS, Over 300 girls and women have been murdered in Juarez over the last 10 years, one third of them raped and mutilated before death, and several of them El Pasoans; and

WHEREAS, Interpersonal and street violence is problematic in Juarez for both men and women, with the most recent example being backyard burials in early 2004; and

WHEREAS, Disappearances of people are also problematic in Juarez, affecting El Pasoans, their relatives and friends; and

WHEREAS, Worldwide, women face special safety threats in their homes and on the streets, whether from domestic violence, rape, and/or serial killers, with an average of 2,400 domestic violence calls per month reported to the police in El Paso.

NOW THEREFORE, BE IT PROCLAIMED by the Mayor and Council February 14, 2004 shall be known as:

"VDAY, ANTI-VIOLENCE DAY"

BE IT FURTHER RESOLVED, that the El Paso City Council supports Bi-national cooperation to call attention to the problems and encourages work towards Bi-national solutions including recognition of human rights.

In Witness Whereof, I have hereunto set my hand and caused the official seal of the City of El Paso to be affixed this 14th day of February A.D., 20 04.

Mayor
Joe Wardy

Chapter 5

GOVERNMENT RESPONSES TO VIOLENCE AGAINST WOMEN

"If you don't do what I tell you, I am going to take you to Juarez and shoot you in the desert." We have had a couple of clients whose partners have taken them into Mexico and just abandoned them in the desert.

—GLORIA TERRY OF EL PASO CENTER AGAINST FAMILY VIOLENCE (IN M. GARCÍA 2004)

Family violence is a driving force for a lot of our stats.

—RICHARD WILES, EL PASO POLICE CHIEF (IN BORUNDA 2005C)

Activists can raise awareness, and nonprofit staff can offer counseling and shelter, but neither group is equipped to intervene in conflict, to investigate and prosecute crimes, or to protect public safety in homes and streets. Those tasks belong to police forces, prosecutors, and the criminal justice system, institutions embedded in the state. In this chapter I offer another perspective on comparative institutions that respond to violence against women in flawed ways, threatening women's lives and safety. Ideally, criminal justice enforcement institutions operate under the rule of law with professional police work, investigation, fair procedures, and an independent judiciary biased neither toward nor against prosecution.

The border complicates law and law enforcement, for different legal systems prevail in two sovereign countries: on one side, local law enforcers of state law and on the other, state law enforcers; one side with a bias against prosecution and the other side with a bias toward prosecution. On both sides of the border, domestic violence and homicide cases must work their way through bureaucratic tangles and delays. But on one side of the border, the "rule of law" is a misnomer (AI 2003; Bailey and Chabat 2002a; Domingo 1999; S. García 2005; HRW 1999; Magaloni and Zepeda 2004). Whichever the side of the border one addresses, political will is essential to enforce laws about violence against women. Still, binational solutions are essential, for borders are porous: batterers and murderers cross to escape the law, and victims/survivors cross for shelter. In Ciudad Juárez, political will and law enforcement institutions are weak in a system where crimes against women are trivialized and normalized.

Law enforcement on violence against women has evolved in two federal systems with different interpretations of federalism in complex, partisan political institutions. First we will look at the Americas generally, its police, and its public safety problems and then at the history of law enforcement on violence against women, a longer history in the United States than in Mexico. Among the questions surrounding interventions are whether activists and professionals should aim for replication and if so, whether South to North, North to South, and/or binationally. Finally, contemporary criminal justice practices are examined with their strengths and flaws. I also analyze sex offender registries, an increasingly common U.S. strategy that both evokes and contains fear but puts potential victims at risk. Symbolic politics and gender performance operate in government rhetoric and institutional practices.

POLITICAL INSTITUTIONS

Mexico and the United States call themselves democracies. Historically, one can raise questions about the extent of democracy for and with women. Political institutions make a difference. Authorities and decision makers operate at different strategic places in federal systems—national, regional/state, and local/municipal. Those who aim to engage with government, whether NGOs or movements, must target their attention to appropriate levels.

Federalism in Different Democracies

Former U.S. House of Representatives Speaker Tip O'Neill once said that all politics is local, but he was referring to the United States and its particular form of federalism. Not surprisingly, U.S. anti-violence activists target much of their attention to local and state governments: the city and its police department; the county and its sheriff department; state lawmakers; and government agencies responsible for implementation, some of which are headed by elected officials.

Yet from historical perspectives, the U.S. federal government has played active roles in dispensing incentives for local and state governments to standardize and professionalize the criminalization of domestic violence, particularly with the 1994 Violence Against Women Act (VAWA I) and subsequent acts VAWA II and III.

VAWA set into law various protections, among the most important of them these four: (1) protection against deportation for immigrant women who report citizen or permanent resident partners' domestic violence to the police; (2) consistent treatment for civil remedies—protective orders—across state lines; (3) monetary incentives to state and local governments for victims' assistance and community policing programs; and (4) the entry of known batterers' names into the FBI-maintained National Criminal Information Center database (Valente et al. 2001). The laws demonstrate that activism has prompted even the federal government to address violence against women on many fronts.

In Mexico, anti-violence activists hardly addressed local government, the *ayuntamiento*, and its partisan elected officials: the municipal president and council members (*regidores*), elected from party lists and ostensible monitors of local government. Activists also invested little energy in pressing state legislators, relatively weak and lacking staff, although state law governs crime. In the state of Chihuahua, men monopolize the state legislature, with women representing a tenth of the seats, never the majority necessary to pass laws.

Theoretically, political parties offer activists access points for getting issues on agendas and responsive representatives elected to office. Only since the 2004 Chihuahua gubernatorial election have detailed calls to address femicide emerged on candidates' agendas. But local activists, cynical about political parties and elections, have invested little time in those targets, either. Instead, activists focused attention on the executive branches of governments at the state and federal levels.

As Victoria Rodríguez states in her path-breaking book on Mexico's decentralization (1997): "One can unequivocally say that all serious politics is federal politics" (23). Under a heavy legacy of Spanish colonial centralization, state governors have been strengthened in Mexico's decentralization process of the past two decades. And the decentralization has complicated Mexico's clientelist political system, that is, one based on personal, patron-client ties more than issue ties. Rodríguez (1997) calls governors the "modern viceroys" of Mexico. Chihuahua's governors, from both the Partido Revolucionario Institucional (PRI) and Partido

Acción Nacional (PAN) in two six-year terms each, 1992–2004, devoted little political will to either domestic violence or femicide, as most of this violence is "normal" in their eyes.

Beyond the North American region, global calls have sounded for rule-of-law reforms. Yet these reforms focus more on stabilizing market relationships than on gender-fair law (Nyamu-Musembi 2005). In many countries, the long-standing historical public-private divide, lodging women in the private sphere, allowed husbands and fathers to govern wives and daughters with little oversight except for excessive violence and homicide. Frameworks to understand and change violence against women require that the rule of law embrace female victims and survivors, enabling women to report attacks, to secure quick intervention, and to deter abusers through penalties. Clientelist systems, built on personal ties more than principle, offer special challenges to rule-of-law reforms.

Political Campaigns and Elected Officials

Historically, feminist activists interact cautiously with the gendered state, a set of institutions permeated with male privilege and sustained gender injustices. Moreover, men essentially monopolized elective and appointive offices until the 1980s in the United States as well as Mexico. In the 1970s, reform-minded activists looked with hope to the prospects that more female legislators would expand public policy agendas to include so-called women's issues such as those related to violence, gender wage gaps, and child care that had fallen through the cracks of male-dominated political agendas. The results have been mixed.

In Mexico, feminists' wariness about prospects for state responsiveness to women lingers longer than in the United States. After the Mexican Revolution, the PRI sustained a one-party presidency for seventy-one years amid multiple political parties, none of which triumphed in national elections. Change began at the local and state levels at Mexico's northern frontier.

Partisan Competition

Genuine party competition emerged at the state and local levels in the early 1980s. In several northern border states, including Chihuahua, PAN won victories. PAN gained the municipal presidency of Juárez from 1983 to 1986 but lost the governorship in what was probably a rigged election in 1986. However, its gubernatorial candidate won the state for 1992–1998.

PAN, a conservative party wherein women and gender issues generate little attention, projects itself as the clean party of transparent governance, thus appealing to PRI-weary voters. PAN state governance co-existed with a PRI presidency during the 1990s, and party rivalry undermined prospects for coordinated solutions over the murders. Likewise, PRI state governance from 1998 onward coexisted with PAN President Vicente Fox from 2000 on. PRI gained when PAN looked bad, and vice versa.

As the women murders became visible, PAN Governor Francisco Barrio Terrazas (1992–1998) and other officials publicly blamed the victims and framed the murders as normal in the press conference excerpts shown in Lourdes Portillo's 2001 documentary, *Señorita Extraviada*. The state attorney general and state judicial police hardly prioritized the murders but rather ignored them and contributed to the political climate that proclaimed few consequences for killing women. Barrio's public comments and behavior differed little from those of his successor, PRI Governor Patricio Martínez, in office from 1998 to 2004, the last four years of which overlapped with PAN's control of the presidency under Vicente Fox. The same party competition contributed to inaction and denial.

Yet PAN President Fox, perhaps responsive to persistent pleas from NGOs and victims' families and the growing binational and international pressure around police impunity over femicide, expanded jurisdiction on the possible violation of federal laws over alleged organ-harvest murders. Thus, he advanced past the previous defensive position that crime was a state and local issue in the federal system of governance. In 2003, the president sent federal preventive police to Juárez, but they made no dent in solving women-killing or the extensive drug crimes that plagued the city since the early 1990s.

Fox made high-visibility federal appointments of women to investigate and prosecute the murders, partly to decorate masculinist institutions, but the violence did not stop. Mexico's political solution relied on symbols for change: the creation of new offices and coordination mechanisms usually headed by female appointees.

Yet in the 2004 Chihuahua gubernatorial elections, few if any NGOs and activists publicly challenged the candidates during their campaigns, perhaps having grown weary and cynical about prospects for change. In an alliance of convenience between right and left, PAN candidate

Javier Corral highlighted the femicide and his promise of action in stump speeches and on the party's website. PRI candidate José Reyes Baeza said little in his campaign but took immediate action after his victory: he appointed a reform-minded attorney general, Patricia González Rodríguez, and replaced ICHIMU Director Victoria Caraveo, a relief for many NGOs.

Police impunity is not unique to Chihuahua specifically or to Mexico generally. Although a climate of fear abounds in many places in the Americas, binational or international assistance priorities have involved drugs, not human rights.

CITY CLIMATE OF FEAR: AMERICAS AND THE BORDER

Juárez has been labeled a "city of vice" historically (O. Martínez 1978) and more recently (Vila 1994, 2005). Pablo Vila analyzes discourse among ordinary Juarenses who describe their stigmatized city with disparaging images: "banditry, gangs, homicides, drugs, and prostitution" (1994, 94). He cites a metaphor from Carlos Monsiváis, one of Mexico's most famous intellectuals: the border as "the garbage can of Mexico" (95). Yet business leaders work hard and invest considerable sums in Plan Juárez and campaigns to clean the image of the city.

The U.S.-Mexico border is a paradoxical place of lawlessness, coexisting with extensive law enforcement agencies, so much so that it has been labeled "militarized" (Dunn 1996). Much law enforcement focuses on drug interdiction, immigration control, and commercial regulation enforcement. The U.S. FBI has interests in organized crime that transcends borders, as does the Drug Enforcement Administration (DEA) (Neild 2005; USDOJ 2004). Freeman and Sierra (2005: 275) document the FBI's large role in drug investigations in providing training to an average of 1,000 agents in "interview and interrogation techniques, crime scene investigations, and evidence recovery, crisis management, ethics and anticorruption, media relations, police street survival and tactical operations." The focus is on drugs rather than violence against women, even though journalists argue that the two are linked in femicide (Corchado and Sandoval 2004a; Washington Valdez 2005). On several occasions, the FBI ran killers' profiles through databases, although Mexico does not invite sustained assistance in this regard.

Throughout the Americas, rapid urban growth, sharp inequalities, and corrupt police contribute to a climate of fear in cities. Consider the words of Jorge Balán: "Living in a Latin American city today is a terror-filled experience" (2002, 5). While official figures may be suspect, comparative institutional analysis depends on them. According to Pan American Health Organization figures for 1998 (PAHO/OPS 2003), Latin America has the highest homicide rates among world regions (also see Moser and McIlwaine 2004). Within the Americas, Mexico's rate of 19.0 homicides per 100,000 is almost double that of the United States (10.1) (Magaloni and Zepeda 2004, 171).

Homicide is not gender-neutral: far more males than females are murdered, most of them in male-on-male crimes. A startling 97 percent of reported crimes in Mexico go unpunished (Rotker 2002, 7; Zepeda 2002). On viewing crime, the passerby may decide "that it is as dangerous to stop for the police as it is to encounter someone who looks like a criminal" (Rotker 2002, 16).

Residents rarely trust the police in Mexico. In one comparative study, 65 percent of Mexican respondents reported little or no confidence in the police; almost half of the Mexican respondents said corruption is a major obstacle to democracy in their country (Klesner 2001, 127; also see Magaloni and Zepeda 2004, 176, on attitudes). One Mexico City study found that only 17 percent of victims reported crimes to the police, saying it was "pointless" or a "waste of time," while another study reported that 73 percent of people surveyed said police protect criminals or cover up crimes. Of those who did report crimes, 45 percent said "nothing had been done" (Giugale, Lafourcade, and Nguyen 2001, 729). During the 1990s, crime reports increased dramatically, and the state of Chihuahua ranked in the top quartile of high crime statistics (Magaloni and Zepeda 2004, 177–179). Femicide victims' mothers in Juárez report frustration and anger with the police, as did survey respondents in this research. Law enforcement institutions are weak, ineffective, and corrupt in many places, not only Juárez.

Institutional Weakness: La Frontera Norte

The Mexico-U.S. border presents special dangers and attractions, given its locale as a drug trafficking gateway of the Americas. And many "cops" are allegedly on drug payrolls (Payan 2006b). But the police-drug links may be even more complex in eras of attempted reform and cartel resistance.

In sustained *New York Times* print and video Internet reporting, with testimony from victims' families, Ginger Thompson cites the "disturbing pattern of malfeasance by state law enforcement authorities responsible for investigating Mexico's most gruesome murder mystery: the deaths of more than 350 women in this border area over the last decade, including at least 90 raped and killed in similar ways" (2005a). In clear language, she discusses police "incompetence, corruption or a lurid connection" to the murders: "The bungling and cover-ups are so extensive that the police and other officials have themselves become suspected of links to the crimes." Yet border human rights activists often note the efficiency of police (and/or their agents) not in solving crime but in assassinating and intimidating journalists, defense lawyers, and activists.

Police problems appear nearly intractable. Thompson (2005a) likens police corruption in northern Mexico to that in Colombia, where the first line of defense, municipal police, is the weakest. In the division of authority between municipal and state police officers, minor offenses are to be addressed at the municipal level. Yet at the border, municipal crime can be major, given its site as a drug trafficking gateway and the related cartel-linked threats and corruption there. In Thompson's interviews at another border location, Matamoros (2005b), municipal police officers discussed taking bribes, accepting gifts, and carrying unauthorized pistols, but they gave guarded responses on whether they serve as lookouts and hit men for cartels. With municipal police salaries of less than US$100 weekly, police said they use their own money to install equipment and buy vests, handcuffs, and bullets by cross-border shopping at Wal-Mart in Brownsville. On the question of whether a trafficker's bribe was accepted, a police officer asked: "What would you say if a drug trafficker came to you and said: Help me and live. Do not help me and die? . . . I would tell them: I do not want to work with you. But I am not here to fight you, either. They do not pay me enough for that. Just do not bother me or my family" (2005b).

Even if police operated with professional standards in a border free of cartel corruption, public funding for salaries and equipment would still be woefully lacking. While public information is not easily accessible or transparent, criminal justice expert José García cites rough estimates of per capita expenditures in twin cities at the border (2002), showing per capita expenditures at five to seven times higher on the U.S. side than on the Mexican side (311–312). Analyzing 1999 figures, García says the Municipal Police Department in Juárez "was budgeted at about US$23 million, while the El Paso Municipal Police and El Paso Sheriff's Office were budgeted at nearly $120 million," although El Paso has only half the population of Juárez (311). Wages, costs, and buying power differ, of course, so "force structures" (as García calls them) are also important to compare: Juárez had 1,200 municipal, 250 state police, and 40 federal law enforcement officers, while El Paso also had 1,200 local (police and sheriff's) officers along with 330 state police and 445 federal law enforcement officers (312). On both sides of the border, jurisdictional issues complicate coordination among officers at different levels of government.

Gendered Institutional Impunity and Women Appointees

Besides the problems of urban insecurity in the Americas, police impunity in Mexico, low budgets, and acute corruption possibilities at the border, gender also complicates the analytic cauldron. As in many countries, Mexico's male-dominated state institutions exhibit a short history of limited accountability to women and gender equality.

The testimonies and stories that victims' families so often repeat in public forums are wrenching tales of police disrespect, disregard, complicity, and incompetence. The investigation process, if it occurs at all, sounds shoddy and inefficient. People sometimes have to pay to bring files to the surface. Coalition Against Violence participants know a victim's mother who received telephone death threats; her caller ID showed that the call came from the state judicial police.

Justicia para Nuestras Hijas (JNH), a human rights NGO based in Chihuahua City, where sexual murders also have occurred, lists numerous complaints about the authorities in both Juárez and Chihuahua City. The victims' families question whether investigations occur, cite how evidence is hidden and/or fabricated, and complain that they experience harassment and intimidation. JNH (2003) notes the appointment of eight special prosecutors in less than six years, beginning in 1997. The replacement of top-level personnel is a typical appeasement strategy in symbolic politics, but it rarely addresses the institutional reform or transformation necessary for core operations to change.

Symbolic politics produces gender performances that involve officials' numeric challenges to NGO and movement femicide figures and a steady supply of female appointees. During the decade-long attention to femicide, Mexican authorities spent more time challenging NGO summaries on the number of female homicides than reporting on the progress of searching for the killers. And in complex partisan politics, even government numbers changed depending on whether the PRI or PAN was governing the state. The government also tended to appoint women to head high-profile offices in male-dominated criminal justice institutions. Fox made two high-profile female appointments, Guadalupe Morfín as special federal investigator and María López Urbina as special federal prosecutor, to investigate the state judicial police, review cases, and develop special tools for prosecution such as DNA testing.

Morfín presented a compelling analysis of the female murders (2004), criticizing the lack of social infrastructure, police impunity, lawlessness, and drug addiction among youth. The document justified the need for dramatic reforms and for the federal government's social development secretariat, SEDESOL, to invest in programs to address city social infrastructure. With language strong and sharp, Morfín cited Federal Deputy Marcela Lagarde, who called femicide a "crime of the state." Morfín continues in Juárez, but López Urbina was replaced in 2005 with another woman federal appointee after she analyzed the often-scanty police reports, beginning with a sample of fifty and announcing premature conclusions about the absence of serial killings in police records. NGOs called her work *pura basura* (pure garbage). In October 2004, López Urbina charged over a hundred members of the state judicial police with irregularities, but the charges were dropped for all but two. Her monograph-length case studies, published in Spanish and in English, suggest that Mexico sought to appease domestic and U.S. audiences (López Urbina 2004).

The upshot of López Urbina's work was to explain away the murders as normal domestic violence and murder. Current and past governors quickly cited her analysis in defense of their regimes. Governor Patricio Martínez used her conclusions to dismiss serial killing claims: "They're crimes of passion, lovers' squabbles . . . and [less] about impunity" (in Corchado and Sandoval 2004b). Moreover, under López Urbina's guidance, the government declared many cases solved and closed. Ocho de Marzo activist and Casa Amiga Director Esther Chávez Cano wondered why the federal government was still sending investigators (O. Rodríguez 2005). According to Marisela Ortiz Rivera, who cofounded Nuestras Hijas de Regreso a Casa with Norma Andrade, the mother of a seventeen-year old assassination victim, both women appointees give the Mexican government "an easy out in the face of severe international criticism" (2005, 70).

Beyond seemingly careful reviews with high-profile federal appointees, newly appointed state Attorney General González found and publicized other irregularities: arrest warrants buried in scores of files, some more than a decade old, that judges had signed and that were awaiting execution (Gilot 2005a). González is said to be cleaning house, reforming procedures, upgrading training, and replacing old equipment, and the state created a new investigative task force headed by yet another female appointee. Cynical activists wait to see whether these actions produce substance over symbols.

POLICE REFORMS: INSIDERS AND OUTSIDERS

Bailey and Chabat (2002b) discuss the mechanisms that after many decades of police corruption in the United States reduced and contained (though never eliminated) the corruption: "competitive parties, professional norms, federal oversight, aggressive litigation, and a variety of checks" (5). Systemic corruption is problematic in many countries. Neild finds that police forces in Latin America are "corrupt and abusive" virtually everywhere (2005, 62).

During the Cold War era, the U.S. Agency for International Development (USAID) operated police reform programs through its Office of Public Safety, but programs aggravated abuse in the military governments of that era. Under a tangle of bureaucratic coordinative mechanisms, new USAID initiatives developed, under its "Rule of Law" program that began in the mid-1980s (Neild 2005). A WOLA-sponsored study noted, optimistically, that contemporary programs attend to the role of "civil society and citizen participation in ensuring successful and sustained reforms" (Neild 2005, 84).

In early 2005, U.S. Ambassador Tony Garza announced that USAID would provide money to the Chihuahua state attorney general's offices as part of its broad rule-of-law efforts. When he cited a US$5 million grant, a USAID press release on February 14, 2005, praised the effort a year after activism peaked on V-Day 2004. However, little transparency exists about specific project intentions, outcomes, and evaluation measures in a nonexistent or semi-secret document.

The Coalition Against Violence made numerous requests to obtain USAID documents that would specify the plans, projects, and outcomes of the $5 million sum through the U.S. congressman's office but got no response from USAID. After that, the Coalition Against Violence filed a Freedom of Information Act (FOIA) request. Six months later, in February 2006, the USAID response indicated that there was no project, merely "set-aside funds" and therefore no documentation or transparency. Border residents know little about the way the money is being spent, but the public affairs offices of municipal and state police in Juárez increasingly name suspects and specific contexts in crimes, disseminating information to border media. Moreover, media reports discuss police training, corpse identification, and the use of high-technology resources, drawing on experts from elsewhere in the world including France and Argentina. The police are portrayed as professional, yet the murders continue: thirty-one female murders in 2005.

Whether relatively corrupt or clean, police forces in many countries have been slow to respond to violence against women. Mexico is a prime example of these delays, and the border is far from adopting a binational approach. Only after repeated pressure did El Paso and Juárez police departments begin to elevate cooperation over dead women at least to the level of cooperation over auto theft. An international free tip line was developed, and in 2003, a first occurred: local police officers engaged in mutual training to secure evidence at a Juárez murder site (Gilot 2003).

Laurel Weldon (2002) used a cross-national baseline from just three decades past to understand long-overdue government responses to violence against women. U.S. response took approximately three decades as well, after sustained political pressure, to enforce laws with a host of specific federal, state, and local training, incentives, and victims' assistance programs. Yet domestic violence and sexual assault are still common. In El Paso and elsewhere, the police are now trained to provide early intervention, and prosecutors work with victims of domestic violence rather than against them in interventions that reorient and/or punish serial batterers. El Paso's response must be understood in the context of pressure across several decades to produce law enforcement reforms.

U.S. HISTORICAL PERSPECTIVES: SLOW RESPONSE

In the United States, it has taken nearly three decades to develop criminal justice institutions responsive to domestic violence and sexual assault. Much attention has focused on police and prosecutorial practices to intervene for women's safety and protection. But successful prosecution is a challenge, suggesting that abusers and serial batterers can still get away with their crimes. Prevention programs have hardly begun, and U.S. culture, including its fascination with guns, still celebrates and tolerates violence.

The history of response illustrates how pressure from "outsiders" in civil society changes "insiders" in bureaucracies and enforcement practices. Over time, insiders and outsiders built relationships and coordination mechanisms in mutual interaction and feedback. Initially, though, outsiders viewed insiders as suspect, for the "hands-off" power and authority of the state had long perpetuated violence against women without consequence for most batterers and rapists.

In the 1960s, police practices treaded very carefully on the private household sphere and interpersonal violence. As an old saying went, "A man's home is his castle." In courtrooms, the behavior and credibility of the victim seemed to prevail over those of the perpetrators. In her comparative analysis of five feminist service organizations that moved from 1970s volunteerism to subsequent professionalism, Diane Kravetz (2004, 29) cites an advocate who spoke on the early years, before rape crisis centers:

> There were several problems. One was the brutal treatment women got in the courts if they decided to prosecute. Often she was attacked, her character assaulted by the attorneys. The other problem was in the reporting of the rape. At times, the police did not handle that in a sensitive way, and the emergency room didn't know what to do. Often, the woman was alone and without support.

Women's movement outsiders fomented inside changes.

Pressures to Change Laws, Institutions, and Enforcement

The U.S. women's movement is nearly a century and a half old, but during its nineteenth-century manifestation, activists concentrated on legal rights, culminating in the female voting franchise enshrined in 1920 as the Nineteenth Amendment to the U.S. Constitution. In the rebirth of the women's movement during the late 1960s, a broader agenda emerged: job segregation, wage inequalities, household division of labor, reproductive health, and violence against women, with mantras that "the personal is political." Through new strategies like consciousness-raising groups, art, music, and film and protests, rallies, and marches, the movement base broadened. Performance activism occurred then and occurs now.

During the conservative chill of the 1980s, movement activity diminished, partly a result of legislative successes, radical individualism, and mainstream institutions that absorbed movement issues. Popular media and culture both stimulated and delegitimized violence: playing to expanded audiences through syndication, television crime dramas such as *Law and Order* and *Special Victims' Unit* focused on police and criminal justice institutions, domestic violence, and sexual assault. However, Barry Glassner cites studies indicating that crime is much exaggerated on television, thus contributing to a "culture of fear" (1999, 43).

Over the past thirty years, institutional policies and implementation have changed, with retraining and new workplace expectations for police, sheriff, lawyers, and professionals in district attorney offices (Frederick and Lizdas 2003; Iovanni and Miller 2001). Before the 1970s, police responses focused on mediation and/or separation if and when called to address domestic abuse, but they made few criminal arrests. With the racism that infected professional police practices, heavier enforcement occurred within African American and Latino communities.

Another breakthrough emerged with civil remedies that survived constitutional challenges in the late 1970s. In the early 1980s in El Paso, the county attorney began to develop procedures to offer civil remedies—paper protection in the form of protective orders that require abusers to maintain certain distances from the victims. But only if violated are there criminal consequences. El Paso was not the only area with delayed responses. Iovanni and Miller (2001) cite figures from the late 1980s showing the hands-off, conciliation approach that police continued to use. "Mandatory arrest" policies produced just 5 percent arrest rates (305).

Women's movement activists, eager to connect ideas to practice, founded voluntary centers for rape crisis, rape-victim counseling, and battered-women's shelters. While cynical activists expected little response or assistance, gradually these voluntary organizations transformed themselves into tax-exempt nonprofit public service organizations, recruiting professional advocates and providers who sustained their organizations from various sources: government grants and reimbursements for services and private and philanthropic support (Kravetz 2004). Grants from the federal and state governments strengthened these nonprofit organizations and sustained part of their funding. However, potential economic dependency issues emerged (De Santis 2006; see Alvarez 1998 on "NGO-ization" in Latin America). Feminists worried that NGOs would lose their critical edge and autonomy, making compromises on services in order to sustain monetary support.

Nonprofit public service organizations provide counseling, shelter, and medical assistance to victims/survivors. El Paso is home to the Sexual Trauma and Abuse Response Services (STARS, formerly known as the rape-crisis center) and the Center Against Family Violence, which runs a battered-women's shelter serving more than a thousand people per year, and thirty-one other homeless shelters, several of which specialize in providing spaces for mothers and children. The El Paso Police and Sheriff's Departments are staffed with victims' assistance professionals and volunteers. Public and nonprofit staff members coordinate work through monthly meetings. Health professionals have stakes in reporting abuse in an era of "mandatory reporting policies," but one cannot assume that such policies match actual practices.

Re-Regulating Insiders and Professionals

"Law and order" issues generate strong constituencies in U.S. politics. Even with backlash against the women's movement and threats to pro-active government with cuts in social services funding, law and order issues have bipartisan support, with crime-reduction programs appealing to many. Public safety expenses consume a large share of local government (about two-thirds of El Paso city and county budgets). Even Texas, with a political culture of limited government and a low social service budgetary ranking among states, provides financial support through crime victims' compensation with elaborate but fair procedures, about which police and victims' staff are well versed and trained. Victims' advocates augment broad-based bipartisan political support for insiders and outsiders as they interact with law enforcement agencies. Subject to a barrage of crime news highlighting crime in everyday life, the broad public is likely to sustain its commitment to law and order issues. Universities and community colleges mainstream the study of criminal justice and criminology programs, and extensive research and data collection make crime visible to the wider public. Gradually, professionals in the criminal justice system began to see connections among family violence, sexual assault, and other crime statistics by which their work and institutions are judged.

El Paso's law enforcement leaders—District Attorney Jaime Esparza and Police Chief Richard Wiles—reiterate the problem of extensive domestic violence crimes. In government agencies with open and transparent accountability for their performance, numeric metaphors matter with meanings that are more than symbolic. Police Chief Wiles speaks openly of the challenges to the department: "Domestic violence is 50 percent of our assaults. What we find is, you are more likely to get injured in your home by someone you know than a stranger" (in Borunda 2005c).

Like drunk drivers, El Pasoans charged with domestic assault have their photos posted on the Police Department website for two weeks, a way to shame offenders. But batterers with low stakes in conformity (unemployment, casual work, unstable housing, arrest records, etc.) have

El Paso Police Department regional office wall commemorates officers killed while on duty. The officer in the center photo was killed while responding to a domestic violence call in 2004. (Kathleen Staudt)

little reason to care about public image and little incentive to comply with laws, protective orders, and other bureaucratic procedures.

In El Paso, police officers are trained at the police academy and in everyday work in ways that make domestic violence a priority. Officers know that domestic violence calls are among the most dangerous. When I completed my victims' training drive-along stint, ten hours on a Sunday in May 2005, the supervisor warned officers before their shift: Be careful; it's Mothers Day! There will be a lot of "58s" (emergency dispatch code for domestic violence), drinking, disappointments, and so on. At each El Paso regional command center as well as at headquarters, the walls display pictures memorializing officers who died during duty. The most recent was an officer killed at a 2004 domestic violence call in a middle-class El Paso neighborhood with a firearm at the home. His picture on all those walls hangs as both a shrine and a warning.

Collaboration: Nonprofits, Local Institutions

From a once tense, untrusting relationship, NGOs and nonprofit public service organizations began to develop better working relations with local police and sheriff departments. With incentives from federal funding in the mid-1990s, stakeholders inside and outside criminal justice agencies organized coordination councils around domestic violence and victims' assistance. Police and public service agencies recruit volunteers to assist victims and facilitate crime reports and prosecution.

I joined the El Paso Police Department's Victims' Services Response Team in one of several eighty-hour training programs offered annually, with a wide cross-section of civil society volunteers in terms of age, ethnicity, and gender. Trained by a mix of insiders and outsiders, we all committed to monthly shifts for victims' assistance work. I also participated in several law enforcement joint training exercises in which public and nonprofit staff members hear experts discuss institutional "best practices" for reducing domestic violence and prosecuting cases. At one, University of Texas law school feminist professor Sarah Buehl presented theoretically sharp and focused training with concrete strategies from other local institutions around the country to an audience of two hundred, including the police chief and county and district attorneys, who stayed for the entire lengthy training. Politicians and the public at least partially judge law enforcement officials by statistics that show whether crime rates are rising or falling.

Criminal justice institutions and nonprofit organizations cooperate on programs focused on men. Another tool in the arsenal of responses to violence against women emerged with the birth and spread of Battering Intervention and Prevention Programs (BIPPs). Courts use such programs in lieu of prison terms, diverting or deferring offenders' sentences (Sadusky 2003). The programs aim to change the perpetrators—the batterers, perhaps more accurately described as serial batterers, so that their relationships are not marred with violence. BIPPs focus on power and control in relationships and on educating batterers to accept responsibility and accountability for a wide range of abuses, from psychological and verbal to physical and sexual. Nationally, program outcomes have been mixed, depending on many factors such as batterers' job and housing stability, previous arrest records, and psychological profiles.

In El Paso, approximately six hundred participants attend BIPPs annually, 90 percent of them men. The program is twenty-six weeks long and involves reflection (homework), group dynamics, and trained facilitators. The Center Against Family Violence adopted and customized the "Duluth Model" for border use in Spanish and English; it is focused on power and control dynamics, generating accountability and responsibility, and only thereafter, techniques for better communication and anger management.

In early 2005, I observed several BIPP sessions with a motley group of men, ranging from working-class to seemingly professional men who appeared to disdain sitting near blue-collar men. Participants shared their homework, for example noting instances of "male privilege" during the week. BIPP facilitators drew on participants' own cases with role-playing that involved the abuser and the victim. I observed scenes ranging from clever manipulators who played the word game to men who warned peers that they lost everything once their families left. One man who gave the "right" responses in discussion just did not "get it" when he performed the role playing. He repeated this twice more without figuring out what was lacking in his response to the role-play "victim" disagreeing with him, all to the evident amazement of the other men in the room.

Community policing strategies over the past decade have drawn on multiple organizational partnerships to prevent and reduce crime. Police officers in the United States respond to domestic violence calls operating under more recent pro-arrest, preferential, or what are euphemistically called "mandatory arrest" laws and policies. Policies, however, are not the same as practices. No matter what the regulatory net, defendants and their attorneys find loopholes, make delays, impugn victims' histories, and work on them to withdraw testimony, perhaps best called "witness tampering" (Buehl 2005).

El Paso documents domestic violence well, for each call to 911 is recorded and counted. Horrifying tapes are played in the Victims' Services Response Team training programs. I can never forget actual calls to 911 that I heard: excruciating minutes passed while the dispatch operator kept the screaming caller on the line as the stalker was breaking in with police sirens heard in the background. In El Paso, 28,000 domestic violence calls to the Police Department occurred in 2004 (including sibling, parental, and partner incidents), but only 10 percent resulted in arrests (Romero and Yellen 2004, 27). Once an incident is reported, a vigorous domestic violence prosecutorial team at the district attorney's office works with sensitivity to victims. To encourage victims' commitment to testify in court, the district attorney's office commissioned production of Spanish- and English-language videos drawing on actual survivors who gave witness in the prosecution of their ex-abusers.

Bias Against Prosecution

U.S. legal tools and machinery sound impressive, but policies' promises are not always delivered in practice the way they sound on paper and can require eternal vigilance from civil society. Many discretionary factors operate at various points of the criminal justice system, where "street-level bureaucrats" (SLBs)—police officers and judges—make decisions with little oversight (Lipsky 1980). Such decisions may be infused with prejudices and assumptions that work either for or against victims and either for or against abusers. And the border offers continual challenges to justice for all. For example, VAWA rules to protect immigrant victims take years to seep down the bureaucracy and subsequently into the hearts and minds of local sheriff's deputies, some of whom threaten families that report violence with a warning: Next time, we'll call the Border Patrol.

In El Paso, county attorneys are elected officials whose offices have professional staff capability to deal with civil remedies such as protective orders (POs). The county-level district attorneys are also elected officials who organize professional staff capability to prosecute domestic violence. In El Paso, protective order requests average 100 to 150 monthly, but approximately 400 are issued annually, for the judges who make the final decisions are "frontline" SLBs with discretionary authority. But even before a judge is involved, the POs must be officially served to the batterers; at this point the process stops for the 40 to 50 percent of abusers who "disappear" by not only changing residences but also crossing the border (Salinas 2005).

Similar bureaucratic delays, negotiations, and loopholes hinder the criminal prosecution of batterers. The usual domestic violence charge is minor—a misdemeanor—but if abusers repeat their offenses and/or use weapons, the crimes are considered aggravated domestic and sexual assault—major felony crimes. After being charged, batterers can be released on bail. Judges, with their discretion, set it as low as $500, resulting in a mere $50 slap on the hand. As elsewhere in the United States, the post-report period is a dangerous time for victims, as perpetrators may retaliate and/or pressure fearful victims to drop charges (Buehl 2005; Iovanni and Miller 2001). To increase conviction rates amid time-consuming and costly jury trials, prosecutors negotiate plea bargains in which defendants plead guilty to lesser charges. In El Paso, most cases are "worked out" ahead of time; it is estimated that 95 percent do not go to trial.

Despite institutional advances, the U.S. criminal justice system involves bureaucratic delays and evidence-beyond-reasonable-doubt standards that make convictions difficult. If victims will not testify in court—whether due to fear, love, devalued selves, or economic dependency—cases are weakened. With lesser pleas, the courtroom drama may be avoided altogether when batterers accept assignments to attend BIPPs under deferred-judgment programs in lieu of jail sentences. Probation officers' ability to follow up is limited by large caseloads that average 150 in the El Paso area. If convicted, criminals are sentenced but escape full sentence terms for good behavior in an expensive prison system where rehabilitation is questionable.

MEXICO: DELAYED REFORMS

In Juárez, law enforcement is primarily a state jurisdictional matter. In Chihuahua, local municipal police are first on the crime scene, authorized to deal with minor crimes, and state police are responsible for dealing with serious crimes. The Ministerio Público investigates and prosecutes crime to judges in closed trials without juries.

Bias Toward Prosecution

In Chihuahua, like other parts of Mexico, if investigation is pursued, there is a bias toward prosecution. Forced confessions are common, and defendants have no attorneys assigned to them. Influential, wealthy people can afford attorneys or evade justice (Freeman and Sierra 2005). Once defendants appear, judges convict them at high rates and sentence them to jail or fines, depending on the crime. For domestic violence, fines depend on whether injuries lasted longer than fifteen days. In Mexico generally, nine of ten suspects are convicted, but experts estimate that only 3 percent appear before courts of law: those caught in the act or unable to bribe authorities for release (Magaloni and Zepeda 2004, 176; Freeman and Sierra 2005, 269). Guillermo Zepeda declares (2002) that "reporting a crime is a trying undertaking," as overburdened officials search for ways to eliminate cases and often blame victims who file reports (89–90).

As for the femicide in Juárez, less than ten convictions have occurred since 1993 for the murders. They include the first serial killer suspect, the late Abdel Latif Sharif Sharif, and the gang he allegedly directed from jail when killings continued. Their sentences ranged from twenty to thirty years, longer than many murder convictions in the United States. A mid-2005 jury trial in El Paso over a man who bludgeoned his partner to death generated a mere ten-year sentence, with good-behavior release likely after five years. With juries, defense attorneys build sympathy for defendants with drinking problems and/or abuse in childhood that exceeds sympathy for dead female victims.

Mexico allows forced confessions, without independent scrutiny of such evidence or jury trials, producing another group of innocent victims. David Meza, a cousin of female victim Neyra and in Chiapas at the time of her death in Chihuahua City, pressed police to solve the murder. When her supposed skull was found with a bullet wound, Meza was tortured in jail and "confessed," even though an examination of the skull concluded it was not Neyra's but rather a man's skull (Ortiz 2005, 68). Meza was released in 2006, perhaps a result of civil society pressure or of the changed political cast of characters at the state level.

Legal Rhetoric: Domestic Violence

Instituted in 2001, Chihuahua domestic violence law uses broad, lofty, all-inclusive language with vision and promise. Chapter 6 of the *Codigo Penal*, Article 190 (translated here by Gabriela Montoya), reads:

> Domestic Violence. Imprisonment from 6 months to 6 years . . . who acts with power or omission with the purpose to dominate, submit, control or physically, verbally, psycho-emotionally or sexually attack any of the family members inside or outside of the household . . . any type of civil or blood relationship, where there is or was a relationship by affinity, marriage, cohabitation or an illegal type of sentimental relationship. (Revised through Decree Number 1038-04 II April 24, 2004) Article 198, Title Ten, under Crimes Against Life and Personal Health allows a fine to be levied of 45 times the person's salary if the injury takes 15 or less days to heal. A lesion that takes more than 15 days is 30–50 times the salary.

Chihuahua attempted to reform rape laws in 2001 through reducing the sentence. Article 239 defines rape as using physical or moral violence to have sex without the victim's acceptance (A. Martínez 2002). Politicians sought to reduce the two- to nine-year prison penalty to one to six years. Women's organizations in Chihuahua, professional and legal groups, protested against efforts to reduce rape penalties. Their shouts, making headlines, compared rape penalties to that for cow theft: "For the government, the theft of a cow has more interest than a girl raped" (ibid., 6). Activists sent letters to state officials and representatives, who repealed the change.

Critics of Mexico's legal process stress the concentration of power in the office of the Ministerio Público, with its limited incentives for genuine crime investigation at the state level for state crimes and federal level for federal crimes. Freeman and Sierra (2005) assert that officials themselves "resort to human rights violations in their attempts to investigate crimes" (267), with widespread torture and confessions as the "queen of evidence" (269). In several femicide cases, police forced confessions in jail by beatings or other torture. According to Magaloni and Zepeda (2004), who judge Mexico's criminal justice to perform poorly, the laws governing public prosecutors' offices (the Ministerio Público) and the police have "tremendous discretion both in the period before a trial takes place and during the trial itself" (175). Few prosecutors proceed to prosecution; two-thirds of complaints to CNDH, the national human rights commission, in 1998 addressed criminal justice enforcement, and half of CNDH judgments rendered involved the Ministerio Público (ibid.). While CNDH can unearth problems and make them public, it has little authority to intervene or change the justice system. In Mexico, citizens cannot file the equivalent of class-action lawsuits against government agencies, a useful tool in the United States.

It is clear that the complaints about femicide join a sea of procedural problems and human rights abuses in the Mexican criminal justice system itself. Compounding these problems is a male-dominated system with a history of little governmental accountability to women. Signs of change are evident amid the symbols and image campaigns of Juárez and the country as a whole.

New Crime Prevention Institutions: Hope for Women?

The state of Chihuahua has developed a new and potentially innovative crime prevention unit: the state Secretaría de Seguridad Pública (SSP). SSP includes the Industrial Police, who monitor the maquiladora parks both for theft and assault. To the extent the new enterprise is more than symbolic, it has the potential to collect crime data, target high-crime areas, and create a safer city. SSP has no equivalent on the Texas side of the border, but both sides incorporate community policing, volunteerism, and youth orientation programs.

In fall 2005 I joined a small group of El Paso anti-violence professionals for a briefing at the new SSP headquarters in Juárez. We walked through a big room with many men working on computers and videos of street scenes shown on wall-mounted monitors. We entered a glass-walled briefing room with state-of-the-art technology. The head man delivered a lengthy briefing, perfected from probable delivery scores of times before, while his male assistants worked other technology. We were shown a short video on SSP programs. As the video was in English, I concluded that the performance was intended as much for Americans as for Mexicans in new public-private partnerships to convey an image (and perhaps reality) of public safety in Juárez.

The video showed examples of the numerous programs in place. Surveillance cameras scanned intersections and possible crime locales around the city and in the maquiladora enclaves. A community-based model sounded promising: residents and businesses would have access to cards with computer chips that allow instant communication to police about impending crime and permit electronic tracking of high-crime areas. Staff members described workshops for women about violence at their workplaces in the maquiladoras. The plan included improvement in street-based policing and increasing performance with better salaries and regulations to curb corruption. Vecino Vigilante (Vigilant Neighbor), perhaps similar to Neighborhood Watch in the United States, was under way, as were in-school programs with police who modeled moral and ethical behavior for the Niño Policía Honorario (Honorary Child Police) program, perhaps like U.S. Explorer programs, a recruitment and training program for high school students aspiring to law enforcement careers. A full database was under development with crime statistics organized by location and month.

One program aimed to transform the culture of violence in the state. The target? Toys of violence. Pictures showed quantifiable success indicators: thousands of these toys, piled high and awaiting destruction.

We began to ask questions in the discussion period. Officials discussed the Alerta Estrella (Estrella Alert), similar to U.S. Amber Alerts for coordinated police action on kidnapped children. But no cross-border Amber-Estrella program was in place. I asked about programs for batterers and counts on women victims of domestic violence assaults. No gender-disaggregated data had yet been entered, although subsequently in conversation officials expressed a willingness to partner over batterer intervention programs, for none existed in the city. Officials talked about changing toward a culture of citizens trusting law enforcement and the justice system enough to report crimes to the police.

On the way out, I asked a computer technician about the previous year's murder count for women; he said three. That was a tenth of those reported in the media and collected in NGO databases. SPP programs sounded promising, but they contrasted thoroughly with the reports of families who are missing daughters or who seek justice through full, professional investigations of their murdered loved ones.

Several Latin American countries opened women's police stations staffed with women and focused on family issues. Such stations are believed to create a friendlier climate for reporting crime, especially for female victims, although their record is mixed (Jubb and Izumino 2003). While Juárez has no women's police stations, the local Ministerio Público office reduced victims' humiliation with separate waiting rooms instead of publicly calling female names in the main waiting rooms.

Some states and cities in Mexico have advanced reforms that make it easier for women to report violence. In 2002, border city Tijuana created a call-in line to record, count, and investigate domestic abuse cases. In a ten-month period, 7,000 calls came in, but only 240 of them (less than 5 percent) moved into investigation. Underreporting problems also occur in Tijuana, as elsewhere, with a Desarrollo Integral de la Familia (DIF) study finding that 76 percent of victims do not report their abuse to law enforcement (Betanzos and Villegas 2002). In Juárez, it is difficult to get counts of domestic violence complaints from public agencies, and in this regard it falls behind other states and municipalities in Mexico. However, in 2006, the local Secretariat for Social Promotion set up a crisis telephone line. And women made 620 of 897 calls, most of them focused on domestic violence (Falcón 2006).

People press, wait, and watch for signs that new preventive policing practices work to increase public safety. But watchfulness and wariness are built on a foundation of mistrust in government. This resembles the cynicism with which activists viewed police reform on the other side of the border some thirty years earlier. The SSP has no program to record and monitor sex offenders, despite offenders' documented presence at the border and their occasional crossing.

SEX OFFENDERS AT THE BORDER

Sex predators are present in all human populations, whatever the ethnicity, whatever the nationality. Most who commit offenses are invisible to the authorities, for many crimes go unreported, as victims feel shame. The immature or vulnerable (especially children) know little about their rights in the legal system. Predators' anonymity allows them to re-offend, perhaps less commonly among registered offenders with pictures, names, and addresses plastered on websites.

Sex crimes have a long history, although in the 1930s, most such U.S. arrests occurred over homosexual "offenses" between consenting adults (Meloy 2006, 34), but a 2003 U.S. Supreme Court decision finally outlawed state sodomy laws (41). By the 1990s, public outrage over sex offenses, long-term damages to victims, and frequent re-offenses generated special responses, including registration and reporting requirements. In an era of "shrinking state budgets" and "prison overcrowding" (8), many states used community-based strategies such as probation, parole, and monitoring systems. Ramshaw reported in the *Dallas Morning News* (2006a) that Texas sex offender registration law was established in 1991, but it has expanded to become "the toughest in the nation," with "zero tolerance" for a range of twenty high-level to low-level offenses that range from sex between consenting juveniles to pedophilia. Lengthy investigation revealed that the Texas online registry system "is highly inaccurate, filled with phony and outdated addresses that permit thousands of offenders to elude authorities and escape public scrutiny"; almost half of those registered in Dallas County could not be located through certified mail and phone calls.

With access to the Internet, it takes only moments to locate registered sex offenders in Texas by name and zip code (at www.texas.gov). Besides Spanish and Anglo surnames and addresses, offenders' race is noted, as are lists of their aliases and pictures. The mug shots are especially interesting because offenders present themselves differently, sometimes only months after their previous offenses: full head of hair in one picture, bald in another; bold-rimmed glasses in one, no glasses in another picture; bearded versus clean-shaven.

When I examined the Texas government website of registered sex offenders for El Paso County in 2005, a pattern emerged. More than two hundred of them lived at two addresses outside local jurisdictions. They lived in a state jurisdiction strip of once low-cost land that the Texas government licensed to the private, for-profit Avalon Correctional Services Inc. based in Oklahoma City. Its website (www.avaloncorrections.com) proclaims that the corporation sustains and grows itself through government contracts. The name of its "halfway house" near Horizon City, the El Paso Multiple-Use Facility, is more suggestive of a community development project than of a sex offender facility.

Figure 5.1 shows the residential distribution of 758 registered sex offenders by zip code in El Paso County. Men make up 99 percent of the offenders. When I examined name, ethnicity, and race and found an overrepresentation of non-Hispanic people in a county that is 80 percent

Entrance sign at the private El Paso Multiple Use Facility housing sex offenders, many of them "imported" from other areas. (Kathleen Staudt)

Hispanic, it became clear that El Paso imported many offenders in addition to its home-grown varieties. These offenders serve out sentences and/or reside in monitored facilities where they acquire jobs in "work release" programs. Perhaps they remain in El Paso for its low cost of living after finishing their sentence and parole. Perhaps also the prospect of border crossing is attractive despite the denial of parolees' travel to other countries. Occasionally media reports highlight sex offenders who have been caught attempting to cross without ankle bracelets (for which state budgetary resources are unavailable). Given the volume of vehicle and pedestrian international border traffic, the likelihood of identifying them is limited unless the futurist scenario (with now-available technology) of tracking chips inserted in their bodies, as has been proposed for temporary migrant workers, is realized.

Sex offender registries amass considerable pools of data for detection once crimes are reported. Registries are not always up to date, as entering the data is a police clerical task that is "not the top priority when resources are short" (Ramshaw 2006a). Certainly, the registries contribute to serial offenders being more easily identified, located, and convicted. I have read of no proposals to post the millions who perpetrate domestic violence and violence against women on website registries. If all domestic violence was adjudicated, that could put nearly a quarter of the adult male population on registries (plus a much smaller percentage of adult women). Currently, Texas registers 46,000 sex offenders (compared to 8,000 in 1999), and the U.S. national registry contains information on 566,000 offenders (Ramshaw 2006a). The Texas registry includes both high- and low-risk offenders, the latter category including under-aged consensual sex partners.

Registered Sex Offenders By Geographical Zip Code

Zip Code	Total	Non Spanish	Spanish
79928	145	94	51
79835	15	2	13
79912	26	12	14
79902	18	8	10
79936	58	15	43
79927	91	42	49
79907	44	6	38
79905	28	3	25
79915	37	3	34
79930	23	6	17
79916	1	0	1
79903	25	5	20
79932	12	2	10
79925	22	7	15
79904	40	12	28
79924	50	23	27
79922	4	1	3
79821	2	2	0
79836	3	1	2
79838	12	1	11
79849	11	0	11
79853	2	0	2
79938	22	6	16
79934	8	5	3
79901	39	14	25
79935	15	3	12
TOTAL	**753**	**273**	**480**

FIGURE 5.1   *Sex Offender Registry Map, El Paso, 2006 (Spanish-surname breakdown)*

While the sex-offender registry provides the public with semi-accurate information, I conclude that it is symbolic, perhaps allaying public anxieties and confirming that government is "doing" something about the problem. However, offenders are at large: some leave the incarceration facilities for work release, and some attempt to or actually cross the border. The Texas government website performs gender in lurid and revealing ways through identifying and exposing potential predators and lulling the public into thinking that one more source of fear is under control. Work-release offenders ostensibly acquire job training, but they work at local fast-food restaurants and gas stations. Nearby residents report that the offenders walk the main streets where school buses pick up and drop off children from surrounding neighborhoods. The Multiple-Use Facility is located three-fifths of a mile from a child-care center. If local school board trustees, county commissioners, and city and town council members had the authority to make decisions on licensing facilities, activists could have pressed for closure, ankle bracelets, and other goals. But distant state bureaucracy authorized the twelve-year licenses for private prison contract facilities in El Paso, far from Austin, the capital, and far from Austin's backyard.

With stronger institutional responsivenss to violence against women in the United States, the historical protection racket for male abusers has been challenged as illegal and as a spur for other crimes. Abusers are costly: to the injured and the children who watch the abuse and to taxpayers for extensive time and money in the criminal justice system. Still, the public is at risk (albeit more fully informed about risks), living at or in the edge of fear.

CONCLUDING REFLECTIONS

Public institutions in El Paso and Juárez respond to violence against women in diverse ways. As in other parts of the United States, El Paso's institutional response over thirty years has improved after sustained pressure from outsider activists, from the state and federal governments, and from insider professionals who collaborate with many partnership organizations and a growing victims' constituency in a community-policing strategy. Budgetary incentives have shaped better law enforcement practices. Yet policy changes are not neat and tidy. Their implementation depends on layers of bureaucracy, street-level bureaucrats, and a justice system biased against prosecution.

Institutions in Mexico have only begun to recognize the problem of violence against women, due to valiant activism from outsiders including and especially NGOs in Juárez. Committed insiders are few and far between, perhaps more visible at the level of national women's machinery and female federal deputies (INMUJERES 2004). Activists are wary of working with insiders, especially the bureaucratic decorations—women appointed to address public malaise more than to engage in sustained reform. Governors, the "modern viceroys," have hardly begun to make violence against women a priority. The federal government could do far more to stimulate and subsidize changes at state and local levels, but the political will has been lacking at that level as well. Minimal institutional reforms have occurred, and if women wait thirty or more years, hundreds more will be murdered and thousands injured in crimes that could be prevented with intervention. Energetic reforms are required to halt the male protection racket that has long characterized gendered criminal justice institutions in Mexico and elsewhere in the world.

Chapter 6	TOWARD ERADICATING
	VIOLENCE AGAINST WOMEN
	AT THE BORDER:
	CONCLUSIONS

Entre los individuos, como entre las naciones, el respeto al derecho ajeno es la paz. *[Between individuals, as between nations, respecting the rights of one another is peace.]*

—BENITO JUÁREZ, 1867

For a Mexico without crime, and for a government committed to a common good

—CALL FOR A MARCH, OCTOBER 2, 2004

This book is dedicated to the problems of and active resistance to violence against women on both sides of the border. In it I have examined domestic violence and as well as female homicide. One-quarter of women experience physical assault at the hands of their partners, and hundreds of women have been killed in Ciudad Juárez, some of them raped, tortured, and mutilated in what is known worldwide as femicide. Violence against women is the overarching problem, requiring institutional response and cultural changes, not the least of which are preventive measures—toward eradicating cultures of violence, of impunity, of misogyny, and of male backlash. Femicide and violence appear to be spreading to (or finally acknowledged in) other Mexican cities and in Guatemala, as well.

CONCEPTUAL FRAMEWORKS

I have used three conceptual frameworks to explain egregiously violent behavior: (1) the global economy, neoliberalism's search for low-cost labor and its iconic Mexico maquiladora model; (2) institutions, both in governance with its weak law enforcement and in civil society activism with its remarkable capacities to frame, dramatize, and disseminate awareness about the horrors of femicide through local and subsequently national and international networks; and (3) culture, drawing from myths, hegemonic ideas about Mexican history, and gender power struggles. All three frameworks contribute to contextualizing, explaining, and perhaps addressing solutions for the stain on the international map that Juárez has become.

Global Economy: Cultural Backlash

Juárez is the maquiladora capital of Mexico, a place that epitomizes global neoliberalism and the inequalities it engenders. It has long been viewed as a city of vice where women are objectified and sexualized. Under the economic model of export-processing industrial production, conditions foment rampant violence against women. The wages of the majority of women and men are so meager that gender power conflicts occur, and male backlash emerges against women as workers and independent beings with human rights.

Gender power relations fall within the cultural framework, but cultures of patriarchy, misogyny, and male control over women are not peculiar to Mexico or to the social construction of masculinity popularly called *machismo*. Yet Mexican myths about female betrayal and rage (recall discussions notably set forth by Octavio Paz) morphed into a national hegemony and added an ugly legitimizing zest to male rage.

What tempers the violence inherent in patriarchy and misogyny? First, governance institutions that prevent crime, protect potential victims, and prosecute abusers and killers. Second, NGOs that challenge impunity. The contrasting female homicide rates—low in El Paso and high in Juárez—reflect institutional strengths or failures.

Institutional quality is stymied with another aspect of the global neoliberal context: relatively free but illegal trade in drugs, as seen in the massive increases in trafficking since the early 1990s. The border region is a drug-trafficking gateway where guns and money overwhelm the rule of law. Drug consumers, most of them in the United States, are complicit in the breakdown of public safety at the border.

Civil society movements are more or less vigorous in exercising oversight on or challenging law enforcement institutions. Strong activism in Juárez, initially against femicide, inspired movements locally, nationally, and internationally to reinvigorate their energies to eradicate violence against women.

These concepts—institutions, culture, and the global economy—all contribute to understanding and explaining violence in the border region. Global economics and cultural concepts enhance insights about the context, and institutional perspectives provide specifics: the identification of deficiencies in police practice along with tools and strategies to challenge governments, their responses, and the lethal cultures that tolerate violence.

Institutions, Governance, and Violence

On one side of the border, there is emergency response to violence *if* it is reported. Interventions can begin as soon as emergency calls are made to 911 and can proceed through a network of public services to provide shelter, counseling, and civil or criminal remedies in a tangled bureaucratic criminal justice system.

The female murder rate is higher on the other side of the border, where violence against women is trivialized as normal, whether it is homicide or less-than-fatal violence and whether it is committed by strangers or partners. Domestic violence and sexual assault rates are high, together suggesting that a third of women are at risk in everyday life. Extrapolating to the city population, these rates amount to around 100,000 female survivors ages fifteen through thirty-nine. These numbers are large, even dramatic, but domestic violence has rarely been emphasized in public discourse until recently. People do not trust the police, and for good reason.

Mexico hosts fine government institutions, but state and municipal police investigative and prosecutorial systems cannot be counted among them, at least not yet. In Juárez, six times more female homicides occur than in El Paso. It is obvious to most perpetrators that they can get away with murder, so much so that some batterers taunt women with such threats.

Abusers and survivors cross the border, from north to south and south to north. They cross to escape the confines of and to take advantage of opportunities in one national system compared to another. Perpetrators cross the border to elude justice, north to the United States or south to Mexico. Consider two cases in 2006 alone. An alleged killer of the eight women murdered—their bodies disposed of at a cotton field inside Juárez in 2001—was living in the United States (Colorado) and upon being charged was transferred to Mexico for prosecution. In another case, the alleged murderer in a 1981 El Paso domestic-violence homicide "cold case" was found in Mexico City and twenty-six years later, according to media reports, will be prosecuted in Juárez under Article 4, a Mexican federal law that allows prosecution of its citizens who commit crimes abroad. These make dramatic headlines. Many more murderers have yet to be located.

Less dramatically, survivors in Mexico resist the violence, endure it, and/or cross to the United States for shelter, as safe places in Juárez are scarce. Survivors have encountered more obstacles since late 2001, when U.S. authorities stepped up monitoring of border crossings for "terrorists." Since 9/11, "border security" has become the rallying cry, but it is a conception of security that hardly deals with the everyday terrors of gender conflicts, domestic violence, and more generalized violence. The narrowly conceived U.S. "security" regime inhibits crossing from south to north, especially for impoverished women without border-crossing cards, visas, or other authorizing documents.

TOWARD SOLUTIONS: ENDING VIOLENCE AGAINST WOMEN

Violence against women cannot stop at borders. The borderline opens opportunities for shelter and threatens justice, depending on whether one is a survivor or perpetrator. From interdependent border vantage points, it is clear that justice cannot be contained within a nation, for crossing produces spillover consequences. The political and criminal justice institutions on both sides of the border must be democratized and professionalized to eradicate violence against women, to hold perpetrators accountable, and to prevent violence from emerging in the first place, beginning with youths, male and female. The border itself needs a binational umbrella for cooperation around human rights and security for people in their everyday lives, including women in their homes.

Binational Beginnings

Currently, sporadic examples of cooperation exist between criminal justice systems in the two sovereign countries, especially since 2003. They include joint police trainings, telephone tip lines, and profile checks for serial killers and sex offenders from state registries and federal databases, DNA, and forensic testing. In 2006, U.S. Ambassador to Mexico Tony Garza circulated electronic messages about binational cooperation to anti-violence activists, citing criminal justice reforms involving the state of Chihuahua's governor and legislature, supported with a US$5 million grant. This is the very money for which the Coalition Against Violence sought clarification with its FOIA request and about which it received a response in 2005 that the project did not exist. This example of a once-closed, now-open initiative shows that transparency in governance is a principle worth pursuing not only in Mexico but also in the United States.

It is difficult to determine how the $5 million is being invested, planned, or used, but sporadic news reports offer insights that raise concerns and quell anxieties. When the money runs out, no longer permitting French and Argentine forensics officers to fly in for skeletal identification, for training programs or permitting New Mexico coroners to render judgments about death (as noted in various media), institutional reforms must be sustained through operating budgets, political commitments, and continuous, vigilant oversight from civil society.

The United States, Mexico, and Canada formalized NAFTA on January 1, 1994, but they have yet to develop a human rights umbrella oriented to safety and the prevention of violence. As the city's namesake remarked in 1867, individuals and governments can work together peaceably and respectfully; they can learn, apply, customize, and/or replicate programs. The militarized model for drug control described by Dunn (1996) is not an effective model for human rights or public safety. For decades, Mexico and the United States have cooperated over drug trafficking, but the track record has been meager and the cooperation leaves little to be desired or replicated in future models of binational human rights protection. Neither is the U.S. sex-offender registry approach a model for future replication and expansion to cover batterers as well, for a registry lulls the public into believing that the particular crime is contained. Registries only enhance detection after new crimes are committed.

Rule of Law on the Border

In Chapter 5 I analyzed the strategies and flaws in law enforcement on both sides of border. Federal government incentives and priority political commitments can change institutional practices, reduce corruption, and professionalize law enforcement at the state and local levels through training and budgetary incentives to increase consistent responsiveness to domestic violence, investigation, and prosecution.

Mexico's "feds" seemed more attentive to investing resources in the appointment of women to appease critics and create the appearance of action than to pursuing nitty-gritty transformation of corrupt state police organizational cultures. The process of reforming police procedures on domestic violence took thirty years in the United States, yet flaws still exist. Delays and discretionary abuses abound, especially in smaller towns and rural areas, under county sheriff rule in Texas. Comparatively speaking, other state governments in Mexico have moved further on institutional reforms than the state of Chihuahua, which remains resistant and mired in organized drug crime.

Mexico's ongoing public awareness campaigns seem promising, such as those in Juárez that condemn abuse including corporal punishment of children. But little attention is focused on men, most often the abusers in domestic violence cases. Batterer intervention programs like those in Mexico City (Gutmann 1996; Liendro Zingoni 1998) and in El Paso aim to forestall the serial battering that occurs when abusers move from one woman to the next throughout their lifetimes.

Economic impoverishment aggravates tensions in households. Women who exit dangerous homes require safe spaces, workforce training, and placement in living-wage jobs where they can rebuild their self-respect. Extended families provide good social capital in Mexico, but migrants to the city have little such capital.

Educational activities that youths have a hand in developing can help build cultures no longer tolerant of violence against women. In Chapter 4 I provided examples of increasing awareness and changing popular culture among secondary and university students through experiential and service learning, dance, music, and drama.

Global Economies, Human Rights, and Local Consequences

At the binational level, human rights institutional protection is long overdue that aids survivors, nets abusers, and sustains cooperation among professionals and activists across and within borders. Close national partners like Mexico, the United States, and Canada ought to work as much for fair trade as free trade, a fairness that would raise wages for women and men alike within borders as well as reduce gaps across borders. Border people share much in common, living together geographically in a radius of just five to ten miles and relating to friends, relatives, and work colleagues. Their regional interests are about more than commerce, low-cost production, and cheap consumption choices.

The current maquiladora model of industrial development creates low-cost jobs that benefit employers and consumers in conditions that exploit workers, grow violence, and generate everyday despair. Artificially low minimum wages breed crimes. Binational human rights–oriented law enforcement will be a costly strategy, one borne by taxpayers on both sides of the border. This high-cost strategy should be complemented with cost-effective strategies to elevate wages, thereby putting resources and choices in people's hands—choices that could deter violence and ease exits from dangerous relationships. North America should do as the European Union does: supply decent minimum wages within the region and flexible labor movement across borders, with region-wide programs and policies to deter violence against women.

Women seek respect, as do men, but the political economy of Juárez generates too little respect for the impoverished majority. Wages are inadequate, hardly decent for urban life. Low wages not only inhibit women's ability to leave dangerous relationships but also undermine men, the minority of whom take out resentment and revenge on their partners. Workers' targets for change should be employers and politicians rather than their partners.

Social Movements and Organizations

Social movements unearthed and elevated patterns of violence against women that increased awareness through claims for human rights, including the right to safety. With widespread media coverage, victims' mothers and activists framed and disseminated their message from the local to the cross-border regional level and the national to the international level. One can only wonder whether social movements, with their emphasis on dramatic performance to mobilize awareness, will sustain their energies and commit persistent dedication to the details of institutional reform, if in fact reform is in process.

As an old maxim goes, "The devil is in the details," and detailed procedural reforms generate little media attention. Nor do procedural specifics and reforms lend themselves to movement frames that allow activists to rouse and mobilize constituencies for rallies, marches, and events. Yet devilish details are essential to monitor institutional transformation. At some point, human rights and feminist activists need to engage with rather than write off details while maintaining their autonomy, distance, and critical perspectives. This may best be done in collaboration with NGOs, researchers, and movement activists. The dangers of what Alvarez calls "NGO-ization" (1998), wherein organizations lose their critical edge with dependencies on public funds, can be tempered with connections to independent feminist and human rights organizations.

An extraordinary combination of people—close and personal networks to distant and impersonal networks—came together to frame the anti-femicide movement. The movement was built on drama and performance, and it depended on continuously horrifying events and shocking numbers of deaths to expand and to pressure governments to change. Movement activists framed goals around killers' dastardly deeds, which continued untouched by law enforcement. In adopting this strategy they augmented the climate of fear and used wrenching, emotional stories to sustain activity. And there is no denying that the deaths are gruesome and the police impunity outrageous in civilized society.

The danger of this single approach to mobilization is that the public will become immune to shock, surrounded as it is with a culture of fear, unless stories get worse and larger death numbers are dramatically conveyed. Another danger of the approach is that people will turn to more dramatic events in other places—places even more exotic than the "others" in Juárez. Some international human rights groups have recently turned their attention to Guatemala, where femicide deaths exceed those in Juárez.

Transnational and international networks are crucial for bringing new assets, contacts, and awareness to horrifying problems at the border. However, once distant networks lose interest, border activists who are engaged with insiders and other NGOs must sustain the interest and carry on. And there is plenty for border activists to do about violence against women, both on the "other" side and in their own backyard.

CIVIL SOCIETY INSTITUTIONS: 2006 AND BEYOND

From the mid-1990s until 2001, victims' mothers and activists in Juárez shouldered the greatest responsibility for continuing valiant attempts to get law enforcement to stop the killings, investigate the crimes, and prosecute the killers. When murderers brazenly dumped the bodies of eight young women in a well-traversed area of the city in 2001, those wretched deeds galvanized activism deeper into Mexico, across the border into the United States, and ultimately to a scale at which "the whole world was watching." Once an anti-war rallying cry, the phrase at the border represented a different kind of war, perhaps termed a "gender war" wherein patriarchal law enforcement institutions failed to engage and respond.

Activists' engagement is broader than it once was, not only in collaborations but also in electoral campaigns. Starting with feminist, human rights, and labor organizations, border activists engaged mainstream populations interested in security: people of faith, in health, and in business, the latter motivated more to cleanse the image of Juárez than its dirty law enforcement institutions. Whatever the motivation, one shared goal is institutional reform for safer homes and streets.

Activists exerted tremendous pressure on governments to respond by using dramatic images, icons, colors, and stories. Distant and local activists networked with one another, strengthening their pressure but at some cost to border accountability and accurate representation. Tensions inevitably arose over who spoke for whom and the distribution of funds raised. One must always remember the mothers' questions about who profits from their pain. Media made visible not only the dramatic activism but also the graphic and grim continuation of murders.

The Mexican government, the main target of pressure, made some concessions, though more symbolic than real. One sure outcome was the appointment of various women to investigate and prosecute the crimes, but all too many of them served as bureaucratic decorations with little authority to render miracles from gendered institutions that long ignored violence against women, even its most brutal forms in femicide. Mexico has a long tradition of cooptation that has generated an equally long tradition of cynicism in civil society about cooptation.

In the 2004 elections for governor of Chihuahua, neither activists nor candidates made demands or promises for reform despite the media saturation around femicide. Yet the new governor made moves toward reform and appointed another woman, this time as the state attorney general.

Some within the business and governing elite seemed ready to use their strategic access to power and the name of a huge nonprofit organization, Plan Juárez, to call for greater public safety and reform in the law enforcement apparatus. For others in the elite, the emphasis was more on cleansing the image of the city, given their worries about investment and tourism.

Among recent establishment efforts, one is almost comical in its approach. In October 2005 the municipal government sought "to break the Guinness World Record for the world's largest hug, in an effort to promote tourism in the city" so the world would know that the city is "peaceful and loving," according to local government financial promotion director Juan Carlos Alonso (González 2005). Other efforts are more sophisticated. In early 2006, business leaders said they would launch a campaign to "clean the image of Juárez" with a documentary to air in the United States, England, Germany, and Japan (Cortez 2006). *Fronterizos/as* hope the elite will cleanse law enforcement institutions and protect public safety rather than just the city's image.

Border Activists: Changing the Mainstream

The federal attorney general's office in Mexico City released yet another report in early 2006, with media fanfare, on high female homicide rates in many Mexican cities. Some activists interpreted this as the usual whitewash but with the slightly altered refrain that many cities are plagued with violence, murders, and women-killing. Some wondered if long-term historical suppression of information on women-killing was finally being publicized. Others interpreted this as a sign that the government was beginning to take violence against women seriously on a nationwide basis. Mexico's respected census bureau issued reports in May 2006 with horrendously high numbers of female homicides in various cities: 1,494 women and girls killed in Veracruz over five years, 863 in the state of Guerrero, and others (*Cimacnoticias* 2006c).

A Commission on Femicide in the federal Chamber of Deputies issued specific recommendations on eliminating gender inequalities, including disaggregated data to diagnose problems and build solutions toward *una vida libre de violencia*, a life free of violence (*Cimacnoticias* 2006c). In fall 2006, the federal Chamber of Deputies published a book, *Violencia feminicida en Chihuahua*, citing some of those same shocking numbers about femicide all over Mexico (Cámara de Diputados 2006). ICHIMU, a Chihuahua state agency, is promoting a new public-awareness campaign. Perhaps the government is finally acknowledging long-hidden, widespread violence against women and the rise in femicide.

Popular culture also incorporates anti-violence messages in many ways, for example on phone cards featuring celebrities (in contrast to photos of smiling people in 2001 government-issued adult educational material).

With analytic hindsight, I conclude that social-movement activists in Juárez and beyond helped to nationalize the issue of violence against women into a broad-based problem to include female homicide and domestic violence. In fact, activists internationalized greater attention to violence against women with their reinvigorated activism at the border, in El Paso and elsewhere in the United States, in Central America, and in international NGOs like Amnesty International and Human Rights Watch that were once less attentive to violence against women. The renewed involvement heightened needs in nonprofit NGOs that assist survivors along with the necessity of prevention programs at secondary and higher education levels. Most communities would do well with such reinvigoration, for the problem of violence against women is not only about the "exotic others" (as Narayan warns) but also about one's

FIGURE 6.1. *"A Home Without Violence" booklet published in 2001 by the Instituto Nacional para la Educación de los Adultos (National Adult Education Institute).*

own community. Fine websites in Spanish and English offer details about continuous violence and continuous shortfalls in the highly discretionary, fragmented, and heavily bureaucratized U.S. law enforcement systems, which are fraught with "intractable, deep-rooted sexism and racism" (De Santis 2006). El Paso's Police Department and district attorney's office perform relatively well under current leadership, but

"If you hurt me, you don't love me," reads a 2006 Chihuahuan Women's Institute brochure.

Phone card featuring TV newswoman Consuelo Duval and the slogan "Whoever hits one woman hits all women," one element in a 2006 INMUJERES public awareness campaign.

that was not true in the past, and future performance always will require feminist-civic oversight.

Activists' accomplishments offer little comfort to the mothers who still search for justice and the prosecution of their daughters' murderers. They continue to mourn, and the benefit of internationalizing and renewing a movement cannot console all their pain.

The 2006 Presidential Campaign

By the 2006 elections for Mexico's president, activists channeled some of their energy into demands—a strategic change from previous elections. In June 2006, broad-based coalitions took out ads in Mexican media and circulated lengthy scripts via e-mail urging presidential candidates to make the reduction of violence against women a national priority. The victor, PAN candidate Felipe Calderón, promised to strengthen the rule of law. The runner-up in the hotly contested race, Andrés Manuel López Obrador, utilized campaign literature with striking graphics on femicide in Juárez, perhaps titillating to some but gruesome reminders to others: a dead young woman with bare breasts exposed and a knife through her heart.

After the presidential elections, lame-duck President Fox announced the end of federal criminal investigations into femicide. In July 2007, President Calderón followed suit, calling for a withdrawal of federal involvement from the Juárez investigations. Action proceeds in the state of Chihuahua but requires eternal vigilance by movement activists. They continue to assess and strategize during this political vacuum over the impending new national cast of characters, while the marches and protests have diminished.

Back to Business and Economics

Activists can and must reach out to broader constituencies to build the critical mass of insiders and outsiders necessary to transform law enforcement and policy implementation. People from broader constituencies, rich and poor alike, have stakes in public safety: to live in their cities without fear. The business community, from small-scale merchants to corporate millionaires, has a stake in fostering a professional police force that works with integrity. Thus far, however, the business community's overall response may be more symbolic than real, as seen in the campaign to "cleanse" the image of Juárez. It is crucial for activists to maintain their oversight of campaign and business hyperbole and dedicate themselves to devilish details in cleansing dirty institutions.

As international activists turned to other places with dramatic femicide numbers, the public learned more about women-killing in Guatemala, where "more than 2,200 women and girls have been brutally murdered . . . since 2001" (AI 2005, 2006, and n.d.). Perhaps there are temptations among some movement activists to switch gears to new "exotic others," from Mexico to Guatemala, or to the next horrific set of numbers about women-killing and rapes. Surely the Darfur region is one that should not pass notice. In Texas in 2005, however, 143 women were killed by their intimate partners (TCFV n.d.). At this writing, mainstream U.S. moviegoers can only wonder how border violence will be performed in writer-director Gregory Nava's film *Bordertown*, due for release in the United States in late 2007, starring Jennifer Lopez and Antonio Banderas. Whatever the representation, Hollywood will engage popular culture. A laudable effect would be for the public to become aroused about the issue enough to sustain it with constant civic vigilance.

Once aware of the complexity of reform, the interaction of people on both sides of the border should occur with mutual respect among peaceable activists who struggle for democracy and good governance.

Individuals and Institutions

Everyone can commit to reducing violence in his or her everyday life. The Alianza Latina Nacional para Eradicar la Violencia Doméstica (National Latino Alliance to Eradicate Domestic Violence) looks forward to a day beyond criminalized solutions, with community-oriented solutions, particularly given the vulnerability of undocumented people living in the United States. The alliance's version of prevention was a theme for its annual conference in 2005: *Yo soy el poder del cambio* (I am the power of change). Everyone is part of the change to end violence in everyday life. Border activists would extend the mandate from "I" to the collective: We are the power of change.

Outreach to and among young people offers promise for the future. In the United States and in Mexico, prevention of violence and the eradication of tolerance of violence are just beginning. Many survivors do not report abuse and crimes against them, and the violence continues. Young people are at the forefront for change—potentially reregulating, Judith Butler would say—attitudes that tolerate violence against women.

People need to work together across age, income, NGO affiliation, academic and activist, institutional, and national lines in binational activism for responses from both governments and our shared binational civil society. Activists must cross the border figuratively and literally, moving from performance to engagement for concrete institutional reform and from the big systemic picture of political will to the details of implementation and enforcement. Far too many sites of violence exist: in households and workplaces, in relationships among adults and with children. Far too many hard-working people, men and women alike, are paid a fraction of the true value of their labors in the global economy.

CLOSING THOUGHTS: THE BORDER AS A SYMBOL

The anti-violence activists who press for responsiveness join a larger movement: the struggle for justice, against crime, and for deeper democracy. Active struggles take place in Mexico, while complacency is common in the United States, even as power concentrations increase in the economic and political establishments. Without active participation from civil society and all the drama of art, film, and music that transforms popular culture, democratic change toward social justice is not likely.

Mexico's femicide symbolizes women-killing and violence against women all over the world. Juárez has become a symbol of the miseries of Mexico. Political scientist Denise Dresser says it eloquently in a 2003 column in the Los Angeles daily *La Opinión* (my translation):

> Ciudad Juárez is a microcosm of the miseries that still afflict Mexico: corruption, violence against women, and the growing brutality with which one lives in any large city. Ciudad Juárez is a crossroads between the wealth of the maquiladora sector and the impoverishment of those who work amid capitalist success and third-world chaos.

Dresser brings the focus back to economics—the obscene inequalities between the rich and poor of the global economic model that dominates the borderlands. The paltry pay for women and for men generates the conditions under which violence and lawlessness flourish. Women cannot exit dangerous relationships with wages that amount to US$25 to $50 weekly and still support children with self-respect. Neither can men support their children with meager wages with self-respect. Yet Mexican and American corporate managers make thousands of dollars monthly. U.S. consumers choose products based more on price than on whether workers live in decent economic conditions and a safe city. And drug consumption flourishes.

We are all implicated in this recipe for disaster.

NOTES

CHAPTER ONE

1. On non-feminist, post-2000 U.S. human trafficking policies, I thank participants at the American Political Science Association panel on Violence Against Women in Eastern Europe and Russia, August 31, 2006, in Philadelphia. In this book I recognize the multiple forms of feminist theories that exist but acknowledge the common threads among them that critique male domination of women.

2. After the Amnesty International count (2003), approximately thirty women and girls annually have been murdered in Juárez, a city twice the size of El Paso, where the comparable figure averages five, according to media reports and an October 2006 El Paso Police Department communication.

CHAPTER TWO

1. Drawing on 2003 data retrieved from the Inter-American Commission on Human Rights, Rodríguez-Hausséguy reports a homicide rate per 100,000 of 47.1 men and 7.9 women for Ciudad Juárez, 34.9 men and 2.4 women for Tijuana (also at Mexico's northern border), and a national rate in Mexico of 28.2 men and 3.1 women (2006, 2). However, recent data reported by the Mexican Congress as drawn from Mexico's census bureau, the Instituto Nacional de Estadística Geografía e Informática (INEGI), raise questions about the northern border as a femicide outlier (Cámara de Diputados 2006). Comparing 1990–1993 data from the commission to its 1994–1997 data, Rodríguez-Hausséguy also reports a 300 percent increase in male homicides in Juárez (from 249 to 942) versus a 600 percent increase in female homicides (from 20 to 143).

2. On violence against women as male mental illness, Mederos, Gamache, and Pence (2005) provide insights from guidelines for U.S. probation officers who monitor male abusers. In the guidelines, the authors encountered an array of hypermasculine expressions among men with extreme gender differentiation, warped perceptions about women, and loss of power. Guidelines warn of a 75 percent recidivism rate for domestic violence (5). An estimated half of those on probation "do not have serious psychopathology" (and half do). Though not

psychopathological, abusers' serious "personality disorders" (13) vary in severity but exhibit the following characteristics, tactics, and claims (6–7):

- A sense of being victims and having their privacy invaded and rights abridged
- Denial and trivializing ("I just gave her a little push.")
- Good intentions ("I slapped her to calm her down.")
- Victim-blaming ("She deserved it.")
- Loss of control ("I lost it.")
- Provocation ("She pushed me into it.")

If the above assertions and tactics represent the half without serious psychopathology, the psychopathological half of abusers on probation reflect irresponsible and dangerous sentiments and behaviors toward women they encounter.

CHAPTER THREE

1. We incorporated two questions about income into the survey, one on household income and one on women's own incomes. In analyzing the results, it became clear that the second question did not generate different responses. Thus, I could not test the Benería and Roldan hypothesis (1986) on the proportion of household income that women earned and its effect on other factors.

CHAPTER FOUR

1. El Paso Police investigator Andrea Baca made several presentations at local and distant conferences about the importance of methodical collection of evidence. In the most compelling part of her presentations, she discussed a five-year-old El Paso girl who was kidnapped from a Wal-Mart and discovered the next day, a murder victim with a plastic bag over her head on which the perpetrator, a previously convicted sex offender, had left his handprint.

2. *Performing the Border* (1999) by Ursula Biemann is a video essay that focuses on the image of women as sexualized, disposable labor. Two more films that highlight violence against women are *Te Doy Mis Ojos* (Take My Eyes, 2003) from Spain, directed by Iciár Bollaín, and *Sisters in Law: Stories from a Cameroon Court* (2005), directed by Kim Longinotto and Florence Ayisi. Both address intervention strategies: an abuser's ineffective anger management and counseling session in the former and women lawyers and judges in the latter.

BIBLIOGRAPHY

BOOKS AND ARTICLES

Alonso, Ana María. 2002. "What the Strong Owe to the Weak: Rationality, Domestic Violence, and Governmentality in Nineteenth-Century Mexico." In *Gender's Place: Feminist Anthropologies of Latin America*, ed. Rosario Montoya, Lessie Jo Frazier, and Janise Hurtig, 115–134. New York: Palgrave Macmillan.

Alvarez, Sonia E. 1998. "Latin American Feminisms 'Go Global': Trends of the 1990s and Challenges for the New Millennium." In *Cultures of Politics, Politics of Cultures: Re-Visioning Latin American Social Movements*, ed. Sonia E. Alvarez, Evelina Dagnino, and Arturo Escobar, 293–324. Boulder, CO: Westview Press.

Amarizca Murúa, Rubén, writer-director. 2004. *The Women of Juárez*. Play. Los Angeles: Grupo de Teatro SINERGIA, Teatro Frida Kahlo. Performed in El Paso on February 13, 2004, at Café Mayapan.

Amnesty International (AI). 2003. *Intolerable Killings. Ten Years of Abductions and Murders of Women in Ciudad Juárez, Chihuahua*. New York: AI.

———. 2006. "Guatemala: No Protection, No Justice. Killings of Women in Guatemala." www.amnesty.org.

———. N.d. AI Alerts. E-mail.

Andreas, Peter. 2000. *Border Games: Policing the U.S.-Mexico Divide*. Ithaca, NY: Cornell University Press.

———. 2002. "Building Bridges and Barricades: Trade Facilitation Versus Drug Enforcement in U.S.-Mexico Relations." In *Transnational Crime and Public Security: Challenges to Mexico and the United States*, ed. John Bailey and Jorge Chabat, 196–215. La Jolla: University of California at San Diego Center for U.S.-Mexican Studies Press.

Anzaldúa, Gloria. 1987. *Borderlands/La Frontera: The New Mestiza*. San Francisco: Spinsters/Aunt Lute Press.

Arendt, Hannah. 1959. *On Violence*. New York: Harcourt, Brace and World.

Bailey, John, and Jorge Chabat, editors. 2002a. *Transnational Crime and Public Security: Challenges to Mexico and the United States*. La Jolla: University of California at San Diego Center for U.S.-Mexican Studies Press.

———. 2002b. "Transnational Crime and Public Security: Trends and Issues." In *Transnational Crime and Public Security*, ed. Bailey and Chabat, 1–50.

Balán, Jorge. 2002. Introduction to *Citizens of Fear: Urban Violence in Latin America*, by Susana Rotker, 1–6. New Brunswick, NJ: Rutgers University Press.

Bartra, Roger. 1992. *The Cage of Melancholy: Identity and Metamorphosis in the Mexican Character*. New Brunswick, NJ: Rutgers University Press.

Baumgardner, Jennifer, and Amy Richards. 2005. *Grassroots: A Field Guide for Feminist Activism*. New York: Farrar, Straus, and Giroux.

Behar, Ruth. 1993. *Translated Woman: Crossing the Border with Esperanza's Story*. Boston: Beacon.

Belausteguigoitia, Marisa. 2004. "Naming the Cinderellas of Development: Violence and Women's Autonomy in Mexico." *Development* 47, no. 1: 64–72.

Benería, Lourdes, and Martha Roldán. 1986. *The Crossroads of Class and Gender: Industrial Homework, Subcontracting, and Household Dynamics in Mexico City*. Chicago: University of Chicago Press.

Benford, Robert D. 1992. "Dramaturgy and Social Movements: The Social Construction and Communication of Power." *Sociological Inquiry* 62, no. 1:36–55.

———. 1997. "An Insider's Critique of the Social Movement Framing Perspective." *Sociological Inquiry* 67, no. 4:409–430.

Benítez, Rohry, Adriana Candia, Patricia Cabrera, Guadalupe de la Mora, Josefina Martínez, Isabel Velásquez, and Ramona Ortiz. 1999. *El silencio que la voz de todas quiebra: Mujeres y víctimas de Ciudad Juárez*. Chihuahua, Mexico: Azar.

Betanzos, Said, and Manuel Villegas. 2002. "Tijuana and Mexicali Domestic Abuse." *(Tijuana) Frontera*, November 11.

Bhabha, Homi. 1994. "Narrating the Nation." In *Nationalism*, ed. John Hutchison and Anthony D. Smith, 306–312. New York: Oxford University Press.

Biemann, Ursula. 1999. *Performing the Border*. Video essay.

———. 2002. "Performing the Border: On Gender, Transnational Bodies, and Technology." In *Globalization on the Line: Culture, Capital, and Citizenship at U.S. Borders*, ed. Claudia Sadowski-Smith, 99–118. New York: Palgrave.

Bojar, Karen, and Nancy A. Naples. 2002. "Introduction: Teaching Feminist Activism Experientially." In *Teaching Feminist Activism: Strategies from the Field*, ed. Nancy A. Naples and Karen Bojar, 1–8. New York: Routledge.

Borunda, Daniel. 2005a. "El Paso Crime Falls for Fifth Year." *El Paso Times*.

———. 2005b. "Run for the Border. Line is Lure for Suspects." *El Paso Times*, February 19.

———. 2005c. "Curbing Domestic Violence: Police Chase 1,000 Wanted on Warrants." *El Paso Times*, February 28.

Bowden, Charles. 2002. *Down by the River: Drugs, Money, Murders, and Families*. New York: Simon and Schuster.

Brandes, Stanley. 2003. "Drink Abstinence and Male Identity in Mexico City." In *Changing Men and Masculinities in Latin America*, ed. Matthew C. Gutmann, 153–178. Durham, NC: Duke University Press.

Buehl, Sarah. 2005. "Effective Domestic Violence Interventions: A Blueprint for Promising Practices." Training, El Paso Domestic Violence Prevention Commission, El Paso County Courthouse, El Paso, TX, August 3.

Burnett, John. 2004. "Chasing the Ghouls: The Juarez Serial Murders and a Reporter Who Won't Let Go." *Columbia Journalism Review* 2 (March/April). Online at http://cjrarchives.org/issues/2004/2/burnett-mexico.asp.

Butler, Judith. 2004. *Undoing Gender*. New York: Routledge.

Buvinic, Mayra, Andrew Morrison, and Michael Shifter. 1999. "Violence in the Americas: A Framework for Action." In *Too Close to Home: Domestic Violence in the Americas*, ed. Andrew Morrison and Loreto Biehl, 3–33. Washington, DC: InterAmerican Development Bank.

Cadena-Roa, Jorge. 2005. "Strategic Framing, Emotions, and Superbarrio—Mexico City's Masked Crusader." In *Frames of Protest: Social Movements and the Framing Perspective*, ed. Hank Johnston and John Noakes, 69–86. Lanham, MD: Rowman and Littlefield.

Cámara de Diputados. See under Mexico.

Camp, Roderic Ai, ed. 2001. *Citizen Views of Democracy in Latin America*. Pittsburgh: University of Pittsburgh Press.

Campbell, Howard. 2005. "Drug Trafficking Stories: Everyday Forms of Narco-Folklore on the U.S.-Mexico Border." *International Journal of Drug Policy* 16, no. 5 (October): 326–333.

Carmona García, Lilia, Elizabeth Aguirre Armendáriz, y Jesús Humberto Burciaga Robles. 2005. "Violencia Contra la Mujer: Frecuencia y Distribución." Unpublished paper. Ciudad Juárez: Universidad Autónoma de Ciudad Juárez.

Chabal, Patrick, and Jean Pascal Daloz. 2006. *Culture Troubles: Politics and the Interpretation of Meaning*. Chicago: University of Chicago Press.

Chant, Sylvia, and Matthew Gutmann. 2000. *Mainstreaming Men into Gender and Development: Debates, Reflections, and Experiences*. London: Oxfam.

Chapa, Sergio. 2004. "Border Violence Takes Toll on Journalists." *Newspaper Tree*, www.newspapertree.com, reprinted from *Brownsville (Texas) Herald*, November 20.

Chappell, Louise. 2006. "Comparing Political Institutions: Revealing the Gendered "Logic of Appropriateness"." *Politics and Gender* 2, no. 2 (June): 223–234.

Chávez Cano, Esther. 2002. "Murdered Women of Juárez." In *Puro Border: Dispatches, Snapshots, and Graffiti from La Frontera*, ed. Luis Humberto Crosthaite, John William Byrd, and Bobby Byrd, 153–158. El Paso: Cinco Puntos Press.

Chihuahua, State of. 2004. *Código Penal del Estado de Chihuahua*, Título 8, Chapter 6, Article 190. Ciudad Chihuahua, Mexico.

————, Secretaría Estatal de Seguridad Pública (SSP). 2005. *Cuadernos.* Press packets. Ciudad Juárez: SSP.

Cimacnoticias (Mexico). 2006a. "Rechazan ONG informe de PGR sobre feminicidio." February.

————. 2006b. "Alarmantes expresiones de violencia, revela comisión legislativa." May.

————. 2006c. "Las cifras de la violencia feminicida." May.

————. 2006d. "Recomendaciones de la Comisión de Feminicidio de la Cámara de Diputados." May.

Coalition Against Violence Toward Women and Families at the Border. Archives, 2002–2006. El Paso, TX.

Cohen, Alex, Arthur Kleinman, and Robert Desjarlais. 1996. "Untold Casualties: Mental Health and the Violence Epidemic." *Harvard International Review* 18, no. 4:12–15, 54–55.

Colegio de la Frontera Norte (COLEF). 2006. *Diagnóstico Geo-socioeconómico de Ciudad Juárez y su Sociedad,* coord. Luis Ernesto Cervera. Ciudad Juárez: COLEF.

Connell, R. W. 1995. *Masculinities.* Berkeley: University of California Press.

Corchado, Alfredo, and Ricardo Sandoval. 2004a. "Juárez Slayings: Inquiry Indicates Police, Drug Ties." *Dallas Morning News,* reprinted in (Sexual Trauma and Response Services, El Paso) *STARS Voice* 2, no. 1 (February): 2–3.

————. 2004b. "Mexico to Release Report on Juarez Killings." *Dallas Morning News,* October 10.

Coronado, Irasema, and Kathleen Staudt. 2005. "Resistance and *Compromiso* at the Global Frontlines: Gender Wars at the U.S.-Mexico Border." In *Critical Theories, International Relations, and 'the Anti-Globalisation Movement': The Politics of Global Resistance,* ed. Catherine Eschle and Bice Maiguashca, 139–153. London: Routledge.

————. 2006. "Binational Action for Civic Accountability: Anti-Violence Organizing in Ciudad Juárez–El Paso." In *Reforming the Administration of Justice in Mexico,* ed. Wayne Cornelius and David Shirk. Notre Dame, IN: Notre Dame University Press, pp. 349–368.

Cortez, Mia. 2006. "Juarez Launches Image Campaign." *El Paso Inc.,* January 15, 2c.

Cravey, Altha. 2002. "Local/Global: A View from Geography." In *Gender's Place,* ed. Montoya, Frazier, and Hurtig, 281–287.

De Santis, Marie. 2006. "Mapping the Obstacles to Criminal Justice for Women." *Online Handbook.* Santa Rosa, CA: Women's Justice Center. http://www.justicewomen.com/handbook.

Desarrollo Económico de Ciudad Juárez. 2004. "Economy," "Maquiladora Industry." At www.desarrolloeconomico.org.

Domingo, Pilar. 1999. "Rule of Law, Citizenship and Access to Justice in Mexico." *Mexican Studies/Estudios Mexicanos* 15, 1, pp. 151–191.

Dresser, Denise. 2003. "Mujeres de Negro: Asesinatos en Ciudad Juárez." *La Opinión* (Los Angeles). January 9.

Dunn, Timothy. 1996. *The Militarization of the U.S.-Mexico Border 1978–1992.* Austin: University of Texas, Center for Mexican American Studies.

Duvvury, Nata. 2002. *Men, Masculinity, and Domestic Violence in India: Summary Report of Four Studies.* Washington, DC: International Center for Research on Women.

Edberg, Mark Cameron. 2004. *El Narcotraficante: Narcocorridos & the Construction of a Cultural Persona on the U.S.-Mexico Border.* Austin: University of Texas Press.

Edelman, Murray. 1964. *The Symbolic Uses of Politics.* Champaign-Urbana: University of Illinois Press.

———. 1971. *Politics As Symbolic Action: Mass Arousal and Quiescence.* Chicago: Markham.

Edleson, Jeffrey L., and Andrea L. Bible. 2001. "Collaborating for Women's Safety: Partnerships Between Research and Practice." *Sourcebook on Violence Against Women,* ed. Claire M. Renzetti, Jeffrey L. Edleson, and Raquel Kennedy Bergen, 73–95. Thousand Oaks, CA: Sage.

El Diario (Ciudad Juárez). 2005. "Divas Time: El lado femenino del arte," November 25.

Englander, Elizabeth Kandel. 2003. *Understanding Violence.* 2d edition. Mahwah, NJ: Lawrence Erlbaum Associates.

Ensler, Eve. 1996. *The Vagina Monologues.* Play.

———. 2000. *The Vagina Monologues.* 1st paperback ed. New York: Random House, Villard.

———. 2002. *The Vagina Monologues.* DVD. HBO.

Evans, Sara. 2003. *Tidal Wave: How Women Changed America at Century's End.* New York: Free Press.

Falcón, Erich. 2006. "New Crisis Line Draws Women." *El Diario,* January 3.

Faludi, Susan. 1991. *Backlash: The Undeclared War Against American Women.* New York: Crown.

Fanon, Frantz. 1963. *The Wretched of the Earth.* New York: Grove Press.

Fernández-Kelly, María Patricia. 1983. *For We Are Sold, I and My People: Women and Industry in Mexico's Frontier.* Albany: SUNY Press.

Ferree, Myra Marx, and Carol McClurg Mueller. 2005. "Feminism and the Women's Movement: A Global Perspective." In *The Blackwell Companion to Social Movements,* ed. David A. Snow, Sarah A. Soule, and Hanspeter Kriesi, 576–605. London: Blackwell.

Ferreira-Pinto, João B., Rebeca L. Ramos, and Alberto G. Mata Jr. 1999. "Dangerous Relationships: Effects of Early Exposure to Violence in Women's Lives on the Border." In *Life, Death, and In-Between on the U.S.-Mexico Border: Así es la Vida,* ed. Martha Oehmke Loustaunau and Mary Sánchez-Bane, 61–76. Westport, CT: Bergin and Garvey.

Fonce-Olivas, Tammy. 2006. "Police Say Filing Reports is First Step in Combating Abuse." *El Paso Times*, January 9.

Fontes, Lisa Aronson. 2002. "Child Discipline and Physical Abuse in Immigrant Latino Families: Reducing Violence and Misunderstandings." *Journal of Counseling and Development* 80 (Winter): 31–40.

Fraser, Barbara, and Paul Jeffrey. 2004. "In Latin America the Gender Gap Kills." *National Catholic Reporter,* October 8.

Frederick, Loretta M. 2000. "The Evolution of Domestic Violence Theory and Law Reform Efforts in the United States." Minneapolis, MN: Battered Women's Justice Project (BWJP). http://data.ipharos.com/bwjp/website.

Frederick, Loretta M., and Kristine C. Lizdas. 2003. "The Role of Restorative Justice in the Battered Women's Movement." Minneapolis, MN: BWJP. September. http://data.ipharos.com/bwjp/website.

Freeman, Laurie. 2005. *Still Waiting for Justice: Shortcomings in Mexico's Efforts to End Impunity for Murders of Girls and Women in Ciudad Juárez and Chihuahua.* Washington, DC: Washington Office on Latin America (WOLA). October.

———. 2006. *State of Siege: Drug-Related Violence and Corruption in Mexico. Unintended Consequences of the War on Drugs.* June. Washington, DC: WOLA.

Freeman, Laurie, and Jorge Luis Sierra. 2005. "Mexico: The Militarization Trap." In *Drugs and Democracy in Latin America: The Impact of U.S. Policy,* ed. Coletta A. Youngers and Eileen Rosin, 263–302. Boulder, CO: Lynne Rienner.

Fregoso, Rosa Linda. 2003. *meXicana Encounters: The Making of Social Identities on the Borderlands.* Berkeley: University of California Press.

Freyermuth Enciso, Graciela. 2004. "La violencia de género como factor de riesgo en la maternidad." In *Violencia contra las mujeres en contextos urbanos y rurales,* comp. Marta Torres Falcón, 83–110. México, D. F.: Colegio de México.

Frías, Sonia M., and Ronald J. Angel. 2005. "The Risk of Partner Violence Among Low-Income Hispanic Subgroups." *Journal of Marriage and Family* 67 (August): 552–564.

Frías Armento, Martha, and Laura Ann McCloskey. 1998. "Determinants of Harsh Parenting in Mexico." *Journal of Abnormal Psychology* 26, no. 2:129–139.

Fromm, Erich, and Michael Maccoby. 1970. *Social Character in a Mexican Village: A Sociopsychoanalytic Study.* Englewood Cliffs, NJ: Prentice-Hall.

Fullerton, Thomas, and Roberto Tinajero. 2005. *Borderplex Economic Outlook: 2005–2007.* El Paso: University of Texas at El Paso (UTEP) Border Region Modeling Project.

Gamson, William A. 2005. "Bystanders, Public Opinion, and the Media." In *Blackwell Companion to Social Movements,* ed. Snow, Soule, and Kriesi, 242–260.

García, José Z. 2002. "Security Regimes on the U.S.-Mexico Border." In *Transnational Crime and Public Security,* ed. Bailey and Chabat, 299–334.

García, Mia R. 2004. "Interview: Gloria Terry." *El Paso Inc.*, July 11–17, 14a–15a.

García, Sean Mariano. 2005. *Scapegoats of Juárez: The Misuse of Justice in Prosecuting Women's Murders in Chihuahua, Mexico.* September. Washington, DC: Latin American Working Group Education Fund and WOLA.

García-Moreno, Claudia, Henrica A. F. M. Cansen, Mary Ellsberg, Lori Iese, and Charlotte Watts. 2005. *WHO Multi-Country Study on Women's Health and Domestic Violence Against Women: Initial Results on Prevalence, Health Outcomes, and Women's Responses.* Geneva: World Health Organization (WHO).

Gardiner, Judith Kegan, ed. 2002. *Masculinity Studies and Feminist Theory: New Directions.* New York: Columbia University Press.

Gaspar de Alba, Alicia. 2003. "The Maquiladora Murders, 1993–2003." *Aztlán: A Journal of Chicano Studies* 28, no. 3 (Fall): 1–17.

———. 2005. *Desert Blood: The Juárez Murders.* Houston: Arte Público Press.

Gellert, George A. 2002. *Confronting Violence.* 2d edition. Washington, DC: American Public Health Association.

Geske, Mary, and Susan C. Bourque. 2002. "Grassroots Organizations and Women's Human Rights: Meeting the Challenge of the Local-Global Link." In *Women, Gender, and Human Rights: A Global Perspective*, ed. Marjorie Agosín, 246–264. New Brunswick, NJ: Rutgers University Press.

Gilot, Louie. 2002. "Tough Bridge Checks Snag More Fugitives." *El Paso Times*, January 16.

———. 2003. "Juarez, El Paso Work Together on First Homicide." *El Paso Times*, April 9.

———. 2004. "Juarenses Confront Fox on Schools, Slain Women." *El Paso Times*, September 22.

———. 2005a. "Juarez Warrants Unearthed." *El Paso Times*, March 27.

———. 2005b. "Security Now Juarez Priority for Businesses." *El Paso Times*, May 15.

———. 2005c. "Prosecutor to meet Juarez victims' moms." *El Paso Times*, June 3.

Giugale, Marcelo, Oliver Lafourcade, and Vinh Nguyen. 2001. *Mexico: A Comprehensive Agenda for the New Era.* Washington, DC: World Bank.

Glassner, Barry. 1999. *The Culture of Fear: Why Americans are Afraid of the Wrong Things.* New York: Basic Books.

Godson, Ray, and Dennis Jay Kenney. 2002. "Fostering a Culture of Lawfulness on the Mexico-U.S. Border: Evaluation of a Pilot School-Based Program." In *Transnational Crime and Public Security*, ed. Bailey and Chabat, 417–457.

Gonzáles, Sergio. 2002. *Huesos en el desierto.* Barcelona: Anagrama.

González, Vanya. 2004. "Juarez Police Take Heat from Business Lead." *El Paso Inc.*, June 6–12, 1c, 3c.

———. 2005. "Juarez Hugs To Promote Tourism." Photo, caption. El Paso Inc., October 2–8, 1c.

Gonzáles de Olarte, Efraín, and Pilar Gavilano Llosa. 1999. "Does Poverty Cause Domestic Violence? Some Answers from Lima." In *Too Close to Home*, ed. Morrison and Biehl, 34–49.

Goodwin, Jeff, James M. Jasper, and Francesca Polletta. 2005. "Emotional Dimensions of Social Movements." In *Blackwell Companion to Social Movements*, ed. Snow, Soule, and Kriesi, 413–432.

Gray, Lorraine. 1986. *The Global Assembly Line.* Film. Harriman, NY: New Day Films.

Grissom, Brandi. 2005. "Violence in Families Remains Problem." *El Paso Times*, October 5.

Guillermoprieto, Alma. 2003. "Letter from Mexico: A Hundred Women. Why Has a Decade-Long String of Murders Gone Unsolved?" *New Yorker*, September 29, 83–93.

Gutmann, Matthew C. 1996. *The Meanings of Macho: Being a Man in Mexico City.* Berkeley: University of California Press.

———, ed. 2003. *Changing Men and Masculinities in Latin America.* Durham, NC: Duke University Press.

Hirsch, Jennifer S. 1999. "En el Norte la Mujer Manda: Gender, Generation, and Geography in a Mexican Transnational Community." *American Behavioral Scientist* 42, no. 9:1332–1349.

Huff, Dan. 2006. "El Paso D.A. Jaime Esparza," *El Paso Inc.*, June 25–July 1, 14a–15a.

Human Rights Watch (HRW). 1999. *Systemic Injustice: Torture, "Disappearance," and Extrajudicial Execution in Mexico.* New York: HRW.

Iglesias Prieto, Norma. 1997. *Beautiful Flowers of the Maquiladora: Life Histories of Women Workers in Tijuana.* Austin: University of Texas Press. Translation of *La flor mas bella*, 1985.

Instituto Municipal de Investigación y Planeación (IMIP). 2003. *Radiografía socioeconómica del Municipio de Juárez 2002.* Ciudad Juárez: IMIP.

Instituto Nacional de las Mujeres (INMUJERES). 2004. *Responses to the Questionnaire Sent to Governments by the Division for the Advancement of Women of the United Nations on Implementation of the Beijing Platform for Action (1995).* April. NY: UN Commission on the Status of Women.

Instituto Nacional de las Mujeres (INMUJERES) and Instituto Nacional de Estadística Geografía e Informática (INEGI). 2004. *Mujeres y hombres en México.* 8th edition. México, D. F.: INMUJERES/INEGI.

Instituto Nacional de las Mujeres (INMUJERES), Instituto Nacional de Estadística Geografía e Informática (INEGI), and United Nations Development Fund for Women (UNIFEM). 2004. *Encuesta nacional sobre la dinámica de las relaciones en los hogares 2003.* México, D. F.: INMUJERES. http://cedoc.inmujeres.gob.mx/php_general/muestra_docto.php?ID=100441.

Instituto Nacional de Salud Pública (INSP). 2003. *Encuesta nacional sobre violencia contra las mujeres.* Cuernavaca, Mexico: INSP.

Inter-Parliamentary Union (IPU). 2007. *Women in National Parliaments.* www
.ipu.org/wmn-e/world.htm.

Iovanni, LeeAnn and Susan F. Miller. 2001. "Criminal Justice System Responses to Domestic Violence: Law Enforcement and the Courts." In *Sourcebook on Violence Against Women*, ed. Claire Renzetti, Jeffrey L. Edleson, and
Raquel Kennedy Bergen, 303–327. Thousand Oaks, CA: Sage.

Isaacs, Stephen L., and Steven A. Schroeder. 2001. "Where the Public Good
Prevailed: Government's Public Health Successes." *American Prospect*,
June 3, 26–30. At http://www.prospect.org/cs/articles?article=where_the_
public_good_prevailed.

Jance, J. A. 2004. *Day of the Dead.* NY: Harper Collins.

Johnston, Hank, and John Noakes, eds. 2005. *Frames of Protest: Social Movements
and the Framing Perspective.* Lanham, MD: Rowman and Littlefield.

Jubb, Nadine, and Wania Pasinato Izumino. 2003. "Women and Policing in
Latin America: A Revised Background Paper." Paper presented at the
2003 meeting of the Latin American Studies Association, Dallas, Texas,
March 27–29.

Justicia para Nuestras Hijas (JNH). 2003. Report, photocopy. Ciudad Chihuahua: JNH.

Keck, Margaret, and K. Sikkink. 1998. *Activists Across Borders.* Ithaca, NY:
Cornell University Press.

Klesner, Joseph. 2001. "Legacies of Authoritarianism: Political Attitudes in
Chile and Mexico." In *Citizen Views of Democracy*, ed. Camp, 118–138.

Kopinak, Kathryn, ed. 2004. *The Social Costs of Industrial Growth in Northern
Mexico.* La Jolla: University of California at San Diego Center for U.S.-
Mexican Studies.

Kravetz, Diane. 2004. *Tales from the Trenches: Politics and Practice in Feminist
Service Organizations.* Lanham, MD: University Press of America.

Larraín, Soledad. 1999. "Curbing Domestic Violence: Two Decades of Action."
In *Too Close to Home*, ed. Morrison and Biehl, 105–137.

Lessing, Doris. 1962. *The Golden Notebook.* New York: Ballantine.

Levinson, David. 1989. *Family Violence in Cross-Cultural Perspective.* Newbury
Park, CA: Sage.

Lewis, Oscar. 1962. *Five Families: Mexican Case Studies in the Culture of Poverty.*
New York: John Wiley and Sons.

———. 1963. *The Children of Sánchez.* New York: Vintage.

———. 1964. *Pedro Martínez: A Mexican Peasant and His Family.* New York: Random House.

Liebowitz, Debra. 2002. "Gendering (Trans)national Advocacy: Tracking
the Lollapalooza at 'Home.'" *International Feminist Journal of Politics* 4,
no. 2:173–196.

Liendro Zingoni, Eduardo. 1998. "Masculinidades y Violencia desde un programa de acción en México." In *Masculinidades y equidad de género en América*

Latina, ed. Teresa Valdés and José Olavaria, 130–136. Santiago, Chile: Facultad Latinoamericana de Ciencias Sociales (FLACSO), and New York: UN Population Fund (UNFPA).

Lipsky, Michael. 1980. *Street-Level Bureaucracy: Dilemmas of the Individual in Public Services*. New York: Russell Sage.

Lloyd, Marion. 2005. "Uncovering Mexico's Dirty War." *Chronicle of Higher Education*, September 23, A26–28.

López Portillo Vargas, Ernesto. 2002. "The Police in Mexico: Political Functions and Needed Reforms." In *Transnational Crime and Public Security*, ed. Bailey and Chabat, 109–135.

López Urbina, María. 2004. *Report of the Special Prosecutor's Unit for Crimes Related to the Homicides of Women in the Municipality of Juárez, Chihuahua.* June and October. Mexico City: Office of the Assistant Attorney General for Human Rights, Attention to Victims and Community Services.

Lovenduski, Joni. 1998. "Gendering Research in Political Science." *Annual Review of Political Science* 1, no. 1:333–356.

Lown, E. Ann, and William A. Vega. 2003. "Prevalence and Predictors of Physical Partner Abuse Among Mexican American Women." In *Latina Health in the United States*, ed. Marilyn Aguirre-Molina and Carlos W. Molina, 572–584. San Francisco: Jossey-Bass.

Lozano Ascencio, Rafael. 1999. "The Health Impact of Domestic Violence: Mexico City." In *Too Close to Home*, ed. Morrison and Biehl, 81–101.

Lugo, Alejandro. 2000. "Destabilizing the Masculine, Refocusing "Gender": Men and the Aura of Authority in Michelle Z. Rosaldo's Work." In *Gender Matters: Rereading Michelle Z. Rosaldo*, ed. Alejandro Lugo and Bill Maurer, 54–89. Ann Arbor: University of Michigan Press.

Magaloni, Beatriz, and Guillermo Zepeda. 2004. "Democratization, Judicial and Law Enforcement Institutions, and the Rule of Law in Mexico." In *Dilemmas of Political Change in Mexico*, ed. Kevin Middlebrook, 168–197. La Jolla: University of California at San Diego Center for U.S.-Mexican Studies and Institute of Latin American Studies, and London: University of London.

March, James G., and Johan P. Olsen. 1989. *Rediscovering Institutions: The Organizational Basis of Politics.* New York: Free Press.

Marroni, María da Gloria. 2004. "Violencia de género y experiencias migratorias, la percepción de los migrantes y sus familiares en las comunidades rurales de origen." In *Violencia contra las mujeres*, comp. Torres Falcón, 195–235.

Martínez, Alejandra. 2002. Interviews with state and local family violence officials, Ciudad Juárez. Unpublished independent study, author's archive.

Martínez, Oscar. 1978. *Border Boom Town: Ciudad Juárez Since 1848.* Austin: University of Texas Press.

———. 1996. *Border People.* Tucson: University of Arizona Press.

Martínez, Ramiro Jr. 2002. *Latino Homicide: Immigration, Violence, and Community.* New York: Routledge.

McAdam, Doug, John D. McCarthy, and Mayer N. Zald, eds. 1996. *Comparative Perspectives on Social Movements: Political Opportunities, Mobilizing Structures, and Cultural Framings.* New York: Cambridge University Press.

McCarthy, John D., Jackie Smith, and Mayer N. Zald. 1996. "Accessing Public, Media, Electoral, and Governmental Agendas." In *Comparative Perspectives on Social Movements,* ed. McAdam, McCarthy, and Zald, 291–311.

Mederos, Fernando, Denise Gamache, and Ellen Pence. 2005. "Domestic Violence and Probation." Minneapolis, MN: BWJP. http://data.ipharos.com/bwjp/website.

Meloy, Michelle L. 2006. *Sex Offenses and the Men Who Commit Them: An Assessment of Sex Offenders on Probation.* Boston: Northeastern University Press.

Mexico, Congreso de la Unión, Cámara de Diputados 2006. LIX Legislatura Comisión Especial para Conocer y Dar Seguimiento a las Investigaciones Relacionadas on los Feminicidios en la República Mexicana y a la Procuración de Justicia Vinculada. *Violencia feminicida en Chihuahua.* Mexico City: Congreso de la Unión.

Mexico, Secretaría de Salud. 2001. *La democratización de la salud en México: Hacia un sistema universal de salud. Programa Nacional de Salud 2001–2006.* México, D. F.: Secretaría de Salud.

Meyer, David, Nancy Whittier, and Belinda Robnett, editors. 2002. *Social Movements, Identity, Culture and the State.* NY: Oxford University Press.

Mirandé, Alfredo. 1997. *Hombres y Machos: Masculinity and Latino Culture.* Boulder, CO: Westview.

Moghadam, Valentine M. 2005. *Globalizing Women: Transnational Feminist Frameworks.* Baltimore: Johns Hopkins University.

Moloeznik, Marcos Pablo. 2003. "The Challenges to Mexico in Times of Political Change." *Crime, Law, and Social Change* 40:7–20.

Monárrez Fragoso, Julia. 2002. "Feminicidio sexual serial en Ciudad Juárez: 1993–2001." *Debate Feminista* 13, no. 25:279–305.

Monárrez Fragoso, Julia, and Cesar M. Fuentes. 2004. "Feminicidio y marginalidad urbana en Ciudad Juárez en la decada de los noventa." In *Violencia contra las mujeres,* comp. Torres Falcón, 43–70.

Montoya, Rosario, Lessie Jo Frazier, and Janise Hurtig, eds. 2002. *Gender's Place: Feminist Anthropologies of Latin America.* New York: Palgrave Macmillan.

Morfín, Guadalupe. 2004. *Informe de gestión: Noviembre 2003–abril 2004.* Ciudad Juárez: Comisión para Prevenir y Eradicar la Violencia Contra las Mujeres en Ciudad Juárez, Secretaría de Gobernación (SEGOB).

Morrison, Andrew, and Loreto Biehl, eds. 1999. *Too Close to Home: Domestic Violence in the Americas.* Washington, DC: Inter-American Development Bank.

Moser, Caroline O. N., and Cathy McIlwaine. 2004. *Encounters with Violence in Latin America: Urban poor perceptions from Colombia and Guatemala.* New York: Routledge.

Murdaugh, Carolyn, Salena Hunt, Richard Sowell, and Irma Santana. 2004. "Domestic Violence in Hispanics in the Southeastern United States: A Survey and Needs Analysis." *Journal of Family Violence* 19, no. 2 (April): 107–115.

Naples, Nancy A., ed. 1998. *Community Activism and Feminist Politics: Organizing Across Race, Class, and Gender.* New York: Routledge.

Naples, Nancy A., and Karen Bojar, eds. 2002. *Teaching Feminist Activism: Strategies from the Field.* New York: Routledge.

Narayan, Uma. 1997. *Dislocating Cultures: Identities, Traditions, and Third World Feminism.* New York: Routledge.

National Institute of Justice (NIJ)/Centers for Disease Control and Prevention (CDC). 2000. *Full Report of the Prevalence, Incidence, and Consequences of Violence Against Women Survey.* Patricia Tjaden and Nancy Thoennes. November. Washington DC: NIJ/CDC. www.ncjrs.gov.

National Organization for Women (NOW). 2005. "NOW Demands End to Violence Against Women in Juarez, Mexico." Press release. December 1.

Neild, Rachel. 2005. "U.S. Police Assistance and Drug Control Policies." In *Drugs and Democracy*, ed. Youngers and Rosin, 61–98.

Noakes, John A., and Hank Johnston. 2005. "Frames of Protest: A Road Map to a Perspective." In *Frames of Protest*, ed. Johnston and Noakes, 1–29.

Nyamu-Musembi, Celestine. 2005. *For or Against Gender Equality? Evaluating the Post–Cold War "Rule of Law" Reforms in Sub-Saharan Africa.* Occasional Paper No. 7. Geneva: United Nations Research Institute for Social Development.

Ocho de Marzo de Ciudad Juárez. 2003. "Estudio Hemerográfico." Unpublished list, photocopy.

Orr, Catherine M. 2002. "Challenging the "Academic/Real World" Divide." In *Teaching Feminist Activism*, ed. Naples and Bojar, 36–53.

Ortiz Rivera, Marisela. 2005. "Fighting Femicide in Juárez." *Left Turn* 18 (October/November): 66–70.

Pan American Health Organization (PAHO)/Organización Panamericana de la Salud (OPS). 2003. *La violencia contra las mujeres: Responde el sector de la salud.* Washington, DC: PAHO/OPS.

Pantazis, Christina, and Lois Bibblings, eds. 2005. "National and International Responses to Gendered Violence Against Women." Themed issue, *Social Policy and Society* 5, no. 1.

Paso del Norte Health Foundation (PdNHF). 2003. *Border Report: A Status Report of El Paso Youth Risk Behavior.* El Paso: PdNHF.

Paterson, Kent. 2004. "The Juarez Women's Murders: Mothers Step Up Justice Campaign as a Cover-Up Takes Hold." November 24. Silver City, NM: Americas Program, International Relations Center. www.americaspolicy.org.

———. 2005. "Edith Is Missing Too." *Newspaper Tree*, June 13.

Payan, Luis Antonio. 2006a. "The Drug War and the U.S.-Mexico Border: What does not Kill You, Makes you Stronger." Special issue, *The Last Fron-*

tier: The Contemporary Configuration of the U.S.-Mexico Border, ed. Jane Juffer, *South Atlantic Quarterly* 105, no. 4:863–880.

———. 2006b. *The Three U.S.-Mexico Border Wars: Drugs, Immigration, and Homeland Security*. New York: Praeger.

Paz, Octavio. 1981. *The Labyrinth of Solitude: Life and Thought in Mexico*. 24th printing. New York: Grove Press.

Peña, Devon. 1997. *The Terror of the Machine: Technology, Work, Gender, and Ecology on the U.S.-Mexico Border*. Austin: University of Texas Center for Mexican-American Studies.

Pence, E., and Paymar, M. 1993. *Educational Groups for Men Who Batter: The Duluth Model*. New York: Springer.

Pequeño Rodríguez, Consuelo, and Susana Leticia Báez Ayala, coords. 2005. *Género, feminismo(s) y violencia desde la frontera norte*, special issue of *Nóesis* 15, no. 28 (July–December).

Peters, B. Guy. 1999. *Institutional Theory in Political Science: The 'New Institutionalism'*. New York: Pinter.

Plan Estratégico de Juárez (Plan Juárez). 2004. "Juárez 2015: The City We Will Become." www.planjuarez.org.

Portillo, Lourdes, director-producer. 2001. *Señorita Extraviada: Missing Young Woman*. Film. www.lourdesportillo.com.

Ramos, Samuel. 1962. *Profile of Man and Culture in Mexico*. Austin: University of Texas Press.

Ramshaw, Emily. 2006a. "Losing Track of Sex Offenders." *Dallas Morning News*, October 1.

———. 2006b. "'Sex Offender' Label Makes No Distinction." *Dallas Morning News*, October 3.

Ravelo Blancas, Patricia. 2004a. *La batalla de las cruces: Una decada de impunidad y violencia contra las mujeres*. México, D. F.: Centro de Investigaciones y Estudios Superiores en Antropología Social (CIESAS).

———. 2004b. "Organizaciones no gubernamentales en la lucha contra la violencia sexual y la impunidad en Ciudad Juárez, Chihuahua (México)." Paper presented at the Latin American Studies Association conference, October 7–9, Las Vegas, Nevada.

Rinehart, Jane A. 2002. "Collaborative Learing, Subversive Teaching, and Activism." In *Teaching Feminist Activism*, ed. Naples and Bojar, 22–35.

Robles Ortega, Rosalba. 2005. "Violencia doméstica y resistencia. Un problema de opresión y desafío." In *Género, feminismo(s) y violencia*, coord. Pequeño Rodríguez and Báez Ayala, 129–146.

Rodríguez, Olga. 2005. "Fox's remarks on border slayings draw ire." Associated Press, May 31.

Rodríguez, Victoria E. 1997. *Decentralization in Mexico: From Reforma Municipal to Solidaridad to Nuevo Federalismo*. Boulder, CO: Westview Press.

———. 2003. *Women in Contemporary Mexican Politics*. Austin: University of Texas Press.

Rodríguez-Hausséguy, Myrna Lorena. 2006. "Invaluable Victims: The Ciudad Juárez Feminicide from a Socialist Feminist Perspective." Master's thesis, international relations, Université Laval, Québec.

Rojas Blanco, Clara Eugenia. 2005. "Voces que silencian y silencios que enuncian." En *Género, feminismo(s) y violencia*, coord. Pequeño Rodríguez and Báez Ayala, 15–32.

———. 2006. "The Rhetoric of Dismissal: Theorizing the Fronteriza/Juarenses Political Activism from a Feminist Perspective." Ph.D. dissertation, Rhetoric and Professional Communication Department, New Mexico State University.

Romero, Manuela, and Tracy Yellen. 2004. *El Paso Portraits: Women's Lives, Potential & Opportunities. A Report on the State of Women in El Paso, Texas.* El Paso: YWCA/UTEP.

Rotker, Susana. 2002. *Citizens of Fear: Urban Violence in Latin America.* New Brunswick, NJ: Rutgers University Press.

Ruback, R. Barry, and Neil Alan Werner. 1995. *Interpersonal Violent Behaviors: Social and Cultural Aspects.* New York: Springer.

Ruiz, Vicki L., and Susan Tiano, eds. 1987. *Women on the U.S.-Mexico Border: Responses to Change.* Boston: Allen and Unwin.

Sadowski-Smith, Claudia, ed. 2002. *Globalization on the Line: Culture, Capital, and Citizenship at U.S. Borders.* New York: Palgrave.

Sadusky, Jane. 1994, revised 2001. "Working Effectively with the Police: A Guide for Battered Women's Advocates." Minneapolis, MN: BWJP. http://data.ipharos.com/bwjp/website.

———. 2003. "Prosecution Diversion in Domestic Violence: Issues and Context." Minneapolis, MN: BWJP. http://data.ipharos.com/bwjp/website.

Sagot, Montserrat. 2005. "The Critical Path of Women Affected by Family Violence in Latin America: Case Studies from 10 Countries." *Violence Against Women*, 11, no. 10 (October): 1292–1318.

Salinas, Juan. 2005. "Protective Orders." Training for Center for Civic Engagement, at UTEP, El Paso, September 17.

Salzinger, Leslie. 2003. *Gender in Production: Making Women Workers in Mexico's Global Factories.* Berkeley: University of California Press.

Sanday, Peggy Reeves. 1981. *Female Power and Male Dominance: On the Origins of Sexual Inequality.* New York: Cambridge University Press.

Santos, Cecilia MacDowell. 2004. "En-Gendering the Police: Women's Police Stations and Feminism in São Paulo." *Latin American Research Review* 39, no. 3:29–55.

Scott, James. 1990. *Domination and the Arts of Resistance: Hidden Transcripts.* New Haven, CT: Yale University Press.

Selby, Henry. 1997. Foreword to *Beautiful Flowers of the Maquiladora* by Iglesias Prieto.

Simental, Gabriel. 2004. "Anuncian nuevo plan de seguridad pública." *El Diario*, November 2.

Smith, Jackie. 2005. "Transnational Processes and Movements." In *Blackwell Companion to Social Movements*, ed. Snow, Soule, and Kriesi, 311–335.

Smithey, Martha, and Murray Straus. 2003. "Preventing Intimate Partner Violence." In *Crime Prevention—New Approaches*, ed. H. Jury and J. Obergfell-Fuchs, 239–276. Mainz, Germany: Weisser Ring.

Snow, David A., Sarah A. Soule, and Hanspeter Kriesi, eds. 2005. *The Blackwell Companion to Social Movements*. London: Blackwell.

Solis, Hilda. 2004. "In Search of Justice." (Center for Latin American Studies) *CLAS Newsletter*, University of California at Berkeley (Winter): 3, 18–20.

Spener, David, and Kathleen Staudt, eds. 1998. *The U.S.-Mexico Border: Transcending Divisions, Contesting Identities*. Boulder, CO: Lynne Rienner.

Staudt, Kathleen. 1986. "Economic Change and Ideological Lag in Households of Maquila Workers in Ciudad Juárez." In *The Social Ecology and Economic Development of Ciudad Juárez*, ed. Gay Young. Boulder, CO: Westview Press.

———. 1987. "Programming Women's Empowerment: A Case from Northern Mexico." In *Women on the U.S.-Mexico Border*, ed. Ruiz and Tiano, 155–173.

———, ed. 1997. *Women, International Development, and Politics: The Bureaucratic Mire*. Philadelphia, PA: Temple University Press.

———. 1998. *Free Trade? Informal Economies at the U.S.-Mexico Border*. Philadelphia, PA: Temple University Press.

———. 2003. Testimony Before the Texas Legislature Border Committees, House and Senate, Austin, April 9.

———. 2005. "Anti-Violence, Self-Defense, and Risk Avoidance: A Comparison of Treatment and Control Groups Among Women Aged 15–39 in Ciudad Juárez." Report submitted to the Center for Border Health Research. September.

Staudt, Kathleen, and Irasema Coronado. 2002. *Fronteras No Más: Toward Social Justice at the U.S.-Mexico Border*. New York: Palgrave USA.

Staudt, Kathleen, and David Spener. 1998. "The View from the Frontier: Theoretical Perspectives Undisciplined." In *U.S.-Mexico Border*, ed. Spener and Staudt, 3–33.

Staudt, Kathleen, and Beatriz Vera. 2006. "Mujeres, políticas públicas y política: Los caminos globales de Ciudad Juárez, Chihuahua–El Paso, Texas." *Región y sociedad* 18, no. 37:127–172.

Steinberg, Janice. 1995. *Death Crosses the Border*. New York: Berkeley Prime Crime.

Stevens, Evelyn P. 1973. "*Marianismo*: The Other Face of *Machismo* in Latin

America." In *Female and Male in Latin America: Essays*, ed. Ann Pescatello, 89–102. Pittsburgh, PA: University of Pittsburgh Press.

Stone, Debra. 1997. *Policy Paradox: The Art of Political Decision-Making*. New York: W.W. Norton.

Straus, M. A. 1990. "The Conflict Tactics Scale and Its Critics: An Evaluation and New Data on Validity and Reliabiity." In *Physical Violence in American Families*, ed. M. A. Straus and R. J. Gelles, 49–73. New Brunswick, NJ: Transaction Books.

———. 1991. *Beating the Devil out of Them: Corporal Punishment in American Families*. New York: Lexington.

Strauss, Anselm, and Juliet Corbin. 1998. *Basics of Qualitative Research: Techiques and Procedures for Developing Grounded Theory*. Thousand Oaks, CA: Sage.

Suárez Toriello, Enrique, Guadalupe de la Vega, and María Eugenia Parra. 2000. *Juarenses por una Juventud Sana*. Ciudad Juárez: Salud y Desarrollo Comunitario de Ciudad Juárez (SADEC).

Sugihara, Yoko, and Judith Ann Wagner. 2002. "Dominance and Domestic Abuse Among Mexican Americans: Gender Differences in the Etiology of Violence in Intimate Relationships." *Journal of Family Violence* 17, no. 4 (December): 315–340.

Switzer, Tony. 2004. *Annual Report: Battering Intervention and Prevention Project, Fiscal Year 2004*. Prepared for the Texas Department of Criminal Justice/ Community Justice Assistance Division, Austin.

Tabuenca Córdoba, María Socorro. 2003. "Baile de fantasmas en Ciudad Juárez al final/principio del milenio." In *Más allá de la ciudad letrada: Crónicas y espacios urbanos*, ed. Boris Muñoz and Silvia Spitta, 411–437. Pittsburgh, PA: University of Pittsburgh.

Tarrow, Sidney. 1998. *Power in Movement: Social Movements and Contentious Politics*. New York: Cambridge University Press.

———. 2005. *The New Transnational Activism*. New York: Cambridge University Press.

Texas Council on Family Violence (TCFV). N.d. "Abuse in Texas." www.tcfv .org/about_tcfv/facts.html.

Thompson, Ginger. 2005a. "Corruption Hampers Mexican Police in Border Drug War." *New York Times*, July 17.

———. 2005b. "In Mexico's Murders, Fury Is Aimed at the Police." *New York Times*, September 26.

Torres Falcón, Marta, comp. 2004. *Violencia contra las mujeres en contextos urbanos y rurales*. México, D. F.: Colegio de México.

Turner, Frederick C., and Carlos A. Elordi. 2001. "Mexico and the United States: Two Distinct Political Cultures?" In *Citizen Views of Democracy*, ed. Camp, 157–182.

United Nations Development Programme (UNDP). 2003. *Human Development Report*. New York: Oxford University Press.

U.S. Agency for International Development (USAID). 2005. "USAID Provides $5 Million for Justice Reforms in Mexico." Press release, February 14.

U.S. Census Bureau. 2000. "El Paso County QuickFacts." http://quickfacts.census.gov/qfd/states/48/48141.html.

U.S. Department of Justice (USDOJ). 2004. Statement of Sandalio González, Special Agent in Charge, El Paso District, Drug Enforcement Administration (DEA), Before the U.S. House of Representatives Committee on Government Reform, Subcommittee on Criminal Justice, Drug Policy, and Human Resources, April 15, 2003. At http://www.usdoj.gov/dea/pubs/cngrtest/ct041503.html.

———, Office of Justice Programs, Bureau of Justice Statistics. 2001. *Intimate Partner Violence and Age of Victim, 1993–1999.* Special report, NCJ 187635. Washington, DC: USDOJ.

Valdez Santiago, Rosario. 2004a. "Del silencio privado a las agendas públicas: El devenir de la lucha contra la violencia doméstica en México." In *Violencia contra las mujeres,* comp. Torres Falcón, 417–447.

———. 2004b. "Respuesta médica ante la violencia que sufren las mujeres embarazadas." In *Violencia contra las mujeres,* comp. Torres Falcón, 111–149.

Valente, Roberta L., Barbara J. Hart, Seema Zeya, and Mary Malefyt. 2001. "The Violence Against Women Act of 1994: The Federal Commitment to Ending Domestic Violence, Sexual Assault, Stalking, and Gender-Based Crimes of Violence." In *The Violence Against Women Act of 1994: An Analysis of Intent and Perception,* ed. Nancy Meyer-Emerick, 279–301. Westport, CT: Praeger.

Varley, Ann. 2000. "Women and the Home in Mexican Family Law." In *Hidden Histories of Gender and the State in Latin America,* ed. Elizabeth Dore and Maxine Molyneux, 238–255. Durham, NC: Duke University Press.

Vila, Pablo. 1994. "Everyday Life, Culture, and Identity on the Mexican-American Border: The Ciudad Juárez–El Paso Case." Ph.D. diss., University of Texas.

———. 2005. *Border Identifications: Narratives of Religion, Gender, and Class on the U.S.-Mexico Border.* Austin: University of Texas Press.

Villalva, Luz Maria. 2005. "Diagnóstico de la niñez en situación de riesgo en Ciudad Juárez." Presentation at the Childhood on the Border conference, UTEP, El Paso, June 24.

Violence Policy Center. 2005. *When Men Murder Women: An Analysis of 2003 Homicide Data: Females Murdered by Males in Single Victim/Single Offender Incidents.* Washington, DC: Violence Policy Center.

Washington Valdez, Diana. 2002. "Death Stalks the Border." *El Paso Times,* special insert, June 24. www.elpasotimes.com.

———. 2003. "Ciudad Juárez: Así empezó todo." *La Jornada,* October 31.

———. 2004. "Officers May Share Blame in Juarez Slayings." *El Paso Times,* October 26.

———. 2005a. *Cosecha de mujeres: Safari en el desierto mexicano.* Mexico City: Oceana.

———. 2005b. "Hidden Victims: Deportation threat keeps many battered women silent." *El Paso Times,* February 21.

———. 2006. *Harvest of Women: Safari in Mexico.* Los Angeles: Peace at the Border.

Weldon, S. Laurel. 2002. *Protest, Policy, and the Problem of Violence Against Women: A Cross-National Comparison.* Pittsburgh, PA: University of Pittsburgh Press.

Wilkie, James. 1984. "The Historical View of Octavio Paz: A Critique of the Washington Address." *New Scholar* 9:1–11.

World Health Organization (WHO). 2002. *World Report on Violence and Health,* ed. Etienne G. Krug, Linda Dahlberg, James A. Mercy, Anthony B. Zwi, and Rafael Lozano. http://www.who.int/violence_injury_prevention/en/.

Wright, Melissa W. 2006. "Public Women, Profit, and Femicide in Northern Mexico." *South Atlantic Quarterly* 105, no. 4, special issue: *The Last Frontier: The Contemporary Configuration of the U.S.-Mexico Border,* ed. Jane Juffer, 681–698.

Young, Gay. 1987. "Gender Identification and Working-Class Solidarity Among Maquila Workers in Ciudad Juárez: Stereotypes and Realities." In *Women on the U.S.-Mexico Border,* ed. Ruiz and Tiano, 105–128.

Youngers, Coletta A., and Eileen Rosin, eds. 2005. *Drugs and Democracy in Latin America: The Impact of U.S. Policy.* Boulder, CO: Lynne Rienner.

Zepeda Lecuona, Guillermo. 2002. "Inefficiency at the Service of Impunity: Criminal Justice Organizations in Mexico." In *Transnational Crime and Public Security,* ed. Bailey and Chabat, 71–107.

WEBSITES

Amigos de las Mujeres de Juárez. www.amigosdemujeres.org.

Avalon Corrections Inc. www.avaloncorrections.com.

Casa Amiga. www.casa-amiga.org.

Center for American Women and Politics (CAWP). www.cawp.rutgers.edu.

Center for Civic Engagement. http://academics.utep.edu/cce.

El Paso Center Against Family Violence. www.cafv.org.

Intergovernmental Parliamentary Union (IPU). www.ipu.org.

Justicia para Nuestras Hijas (JNH). http://espanol.geocities.com/justhijas.

Human Relations Area Files. www.yale.edu/hraf.

Mexico Solidarity Network. www.mexicosolidarity.org.

Texas, State of. www.texas.gov.

Texas Council on Family Violence (TCFV). www.tcfv.org.

V-Day. www.vday.org.

Washington Office on Latin America (WOLA). www.wola.org.

Women in Black. www.womeninblack.org.